MYSTIC
OF LIBERATION

TEOFILO CABESTRERO

MYSTIC OF LIBERATION

A PORTRAIT OF PEDRO CASALDÁLIGA

Translated from the Spanish by Donald D. Walsh

ORBIS BOOKS

Maryknoll, New York 10545

The Catholic Foreign Mission Society of America (Maryknoll) recruits and trains people for overseas missionary service. Through Orbis Books Maryknoll aims to foster the international dialogue that is essential to mission. The books published, however, reflect the opinions of their authors and are not meant to represent the official position of the society.

Photographs by Richard Todd and Moura
Photo Editor: Catherine Costello

First published as *Diálogos en Mato Grosso con Pedro Casaldáliga* by Ediciones Sígueme, Apdo. 332, Salamanca, Spain

Library of Congress Cataloging in Publication Data
Cabestrero, Teófilo.
    Mystic of liberation.

    Translation of Diálogos en Mato Grosso con Pedro Casaldáliga.
    Includes bibliographical references.
    1. Cabestrero, Teófilo. 2. Catholic Church—
Bishops—Biography. 3. Bishops—Brazil—Mato Grosso
(State)—Biography. 4. Mato Grosso (State)—Biography.
5. Church and social problems—Brazil—Mato Grosso
(State) I. Casaldáliga, Pedro. II. Title.
BX4705.C215A3313   282'.092'4   [B]   80-25402
ISBN 0-88344-324-4 (pbk.)

Table of Contents

Abbreviations

CELAM, *Conferencia Episcopal Latinoamericana,* Latin American Episcopal Conference
CIMI, *Conselho Indigenista Missionário,* Indigenous (Indian) Missionary Council
CNBB, *Conferência Nacional dos Bispos do Brazil,* National Conference of the Bishops of Brazil
CODEARA, *Companhia de Desenvolvimento de Araguaia,* Araguaia Development Company
CPI, *Comissão Parlamentária Investigativa,* Parliamentary Investigative Commission
CPT, *Comissão Pastoral da Terra,* Commission on the Rural Ministry
FUNAI, *Fundação Nacional Indianista,* National Indian Foundation
MDB, *Movimento Democrático Brasileiro,* Brazilian Democratic Movement
SNI, *Serviço Internacional de Informação,* International Information Service
SUDAM, *Superintendência de Desenvolvimento da Amazônia,* Superintendency for Development of Amazonia
SUDENE, *Superintendência de Desenvolvimento do Nordeste,* Superintendency for Development of the Northeast

"Your mitre will be a rustic straw hat. . . . You will have no other shield than the strength of the hope and freedom of the children of God, nor will you use any other gloves than the service of love."

Prefatory Poem

Letter to Bishop Casaldáliga

by Ernesto Cardenal

Bishop:

I read that in a sacking by the Military Police
in the Prelature of São Félix,
they carried off, among other things,
the Portuguese translation (I didn't know there was one)
of *Psalms* by Ernesto Cardenal.
And that all those arrested were given electric shocks
for Psalms that many had perhaps not read.
I have suffered for them, and for so many others,
in "the nets of death". . ."the snares of the Abyss."
My brothers and sisters
with the goad at your breasts, with the goad at your penis.
I will tell you:
those Pslams have been banned here too
and Somoza said a short while ago in a speech
that he would eradicate the "obscurantism" of Solentiname.[1]

I saw your picture on the banks of the Araguaia
the day of your consecration, with your mitre,
which as we know is a palm-leaf hat
and your crozier, an oar from the Amazonia.
And I've learned that you're now waiting to be sentenced by the
        Military Court.
I imagine you, while waiting, smiling as in the picture

ix

(smiling not at the camera but at all that was to come)
at the hour when the woods turn greener
or sadder,
in the distance the lovely water of the Araguaia,
the sun sinking behind distant estates.
The forest begins there, "its silence like a deafness."
I spent a week on the Amazon (Leticia) and I remember
the banks of trees hidden by tangles of parasites
like finance companies.
At night you've heard their strange noises
(some are like moans and others like cackles).
Jaguar after tapir, tapir frightening the monkeys,
the monkeys scaring off the . . . macaws?
(it's on a page of Humboldt)
like a class society.
An evening melancholy like that of the yards of penitentiaries.
In the air there is dampness, and a kind of DEOPS[2] smell . . .
Perhaps a sad wind blows from the Northeast
from the sad Northeast. . . .
There is a black frog in the black *igarapés*[3]
(I've read), a black frog that asks:
What forrr? What forrr?
Perhaps a flying fish leaps up.
A heron takes flight, as graceful as Miss Brazil.
In spite of the companies, the enterprises.
The beauty of those shores, a prelude to the society that we shall
        have.
That we shall have.
They cannot, even though they try,
take a planet away from the celestial system.

Is Anaconda around there? Is Kennecott?
Off there, like here, the people are afraid.
The laypeople, you've written,
"through the jungle like jaguars, like birds"
I've learned the name of a boy (Chico)
and the name of a girl (Rosa)
The tribe is moving up the river.
The Companies come putting up fences.

Across the Mato Grosso sky move the landowners in their private
    planes.
And they don't invite you to the big barbecue with the Minister of
    the Interior.
The Companies sowing desolation.
They bring in the telegraph to transmit false news.
The transistor to the poor, for murmured lies.
Truth is forbidden for it makes you free.
Desolation and division and barbed wire.
You're a poet and you write metaphors.
But you've also written: "Slavery is not a metaphor."
And they penetrate even into the upper Xingu,
the hunters of usurious bank concessions.
Weeping in those regions like the Amazonian rain.
The Military Police have told you
that all the Church should worry about is "souls."
But what about children starved by corporations?

Perhaps it's the middle of the night in the Prelature of São Félix.
You alone, in the Mission house, surrounded by jungle,
the jungle through which the corporations come advancing.
It's the hour of the DEOPS spies and the Company gunmen.
Is that a friend at the door or is it the Death Squadron?

I imagine (if there's a moon) a melancholy Amazonian moon,
its light shines on the private property.
The great estate not for farming, let's get this straight,
but so that the little farmer won't have his little farm.

The middle of the night.
"Brother, how long will it take to reach Paranará?"
"We don't know, brother.
We don't know if we're near or far away
or if we've already passed it.
But let's row, brother."

The middle of the night.
The little lights of the dispossessed shine on the shores.
Their tearful reflections.

Far, far away laugh the lights of Rio de Janeiro
and the lights of Brasilia.

How *shall they possess the earth* if the earth is owned by landlords?
Unproductive, esteemed only for real estate speculation
and fat loans from the Bank of Brazil.
There He is always sold for Thirty Dollars
on the River of the Dead.
The price of a peon.
In spite of 2,000 years of inflation.

The middle of the night.
There is a humble little light (I don't know just where),
a leper colony on the Amazon,
the lepers are there on the dock
waiting for Che's raft to come back.

I've noticed that you quote my *Homage to the American Indians*
I'm surprised that the book should travel as far as the upper
        Xingú
where you, Bishop, defend these Indians.
What greater homage!
I think of the Pataxó Indians poisoned with smallpox.
Of 10,000 Long-Ribbons, only 500 now.
The Tapaiamas receiving gifts of sugar with arsenic.
Another Mato Grosso tribe dynamited from a Cessna.
The harsh *mangaré* drum does not sound calling to the moon
        dancers,
the dancers disguised as butterflies, chewing the mystic coca leaf,
the naked girls painted with designs symbolizing boa skin,
with gourd rattles on their ankles around the Tree of Life (the
        pifayo palm).
A chain of diamond shapes represents the serpent,
and inside each diamond other frets,
each fret another serpent.
So that there are many serpents in the body of a single one:
the communal organization of many individuals.
Plurality within unity.
At the beginning there was only water and sky.

All was a void, all was great night.
Afterwards He made mountains, rivers.
He said: "Now everything is there."
The rivers called one another by their names.
Men used to be howling monkeys.
The earth has the shape of the breadfruit tree.
At that time there was a ladder to climb to the sky.
Columbus found them in Cuba in a paradise where everything
　　was held in common.
"The earth common like the sun and the water, without *meum et*
　　tuum."
They gave someone a length of cloth
and cutting it into equal pieces he divided it among the whole
　　tribe.
No tribe in America with private property, that I know of.
The whites brought money, the private monetary evaluation of
　　things.
(Shouts . . . the crackling of huts in flames . . . shots)
Of 19,000 Muducuras, 1,200.
Of 4,000 Carajás, 400.
The Tapalumas, completely gone.
The private appropriation of Eden
or the Green Hell.
As a Jesuit has written:
"The thirst for blood greater than the River."

A new order.
Or rather a new heaven and a new earth.
New Jerusalem. Neither New York nor Brasilia.
A passion for change:
the nostalgia of that city.
A beloved community.
We are foreigners in Consumer City.
The new person, and not the new Oldsmobile.

Idols are idealism.
While the prophets were professing dialectical materialism.
Idealism: Miss Brazil on the screen
blotting out 100,000 prostitutes on the streets of São Paulo.

And in the futuristic Brasilia the decrepit marshals
from their desks execute handsome young men by telephone
exterminate the happy tribe with a telegram
trembling, rheumatic and arthritic, cadaverous,
backed up by fat gangsters with dark glasses.

This morning the termite entered my cabin on the side where the
     books are
(Fanon, Freire . . . also Plato):
a perfect society but without one change
for millions of years without one change.
Not long ago a reporter asked me why I write poetry:
for the same reason as Amos, Nahum, Haggai, Jeremiah . . .
You have written:
"Cursed be private property."
And Saint Basil:
"Owners of the common goods because they were the first to seize
     them."
For Communists there is no God, only justice.
For Christians there is no God without justice.
Bishop, we are subversives
a secret code on a card in a file who knows where,
followers of the ill-clad and visionary proletarian,
a professional agitator, executed for conspiring against the Sys-
     tem.
It was, you know, a torture intended for subversives,
the cross was
for political criminals,
not a cluster of rubies on a bishop's breast.
Nothing is profane anymore.
He is not beyond the atmospheric skies.
What does it matter, Bishop,
if the Military Police or the CIA
converts us into food for the bacteria in the soil
and scatters us throughout the universe.
Pilate stuck the sign up in four languages:
SUBVERSIVE.
One arrested in the bakery.
Another one waiting for a bus to go to work.

A long-haired boy falls in a São Paulo street.
There is resurrection of the flesh.
If not, how can there be a permanent Revolution?
One day the Bogota *Times* appeared jubilant on the streets
(it reached me even in Solentiname)
CAMILO TORRES DEAD
enormous black letters
and he's more alive than ever defying the Times.

And they say in Brasilia:
"Do not picture for us true visions,
speak to us of flattering things, contemplate illusions."
The Brazilian miracle
of a Hilton Hotel surrounded by hovels.
The price of things goes up
and the price of people comes down.
Handwork as cheap as is possible
(for them it is not cleanliness . . . the Beethoven Symphony).
And in the Northeast their stomachs are devouring themselves.
Yes, Julian, capital is multiplying like bacilli.
Capitalism, the accumulation of sin,
like the pollution of São Paulo
the whiskey-colored miasma over São Paulo.
Its cornerstone is inequality.
In the Amazon I met a famous Mike
who exported piranhas to the U.S.A.,
and he could send only two in each tank,
so that one could always elude the other:
if there were three or more they all destroyed one another.
That's like this Brazilian model of piranhas.
Mass production of misery,
crime in industrial quantities.
Death on the production line.
Mario-Japa asked for water in the *pau-de-arara*[4]
and they made him swallow a pound of salt.
With no news because of censorship, we know only:
there where the helicopters gather is the Body of Christ.
About violence, I would say:
there exists the violence of Evolution

and the violence that retards Evolution.
(And a love stronger than the DEOPS and the Death Squadron.)
But sadism and masochism are class harmony,
sadism and masochism of oppressor and oppressed.
But love also is implacable (like the DEOPS).
The yearning for union can carry one to the *pau-de-arara,*
to the machine-gun-butt slams on the head,
the punches in the face with bandaged fists,
the electrodes.
For that love many have been castrated.
You feel the loneliness of being only individuals.
Perhaps while I'm writing you you've already been condemned.
Perhaps later I'll be jailed.
Prophet there where the Araguaia and the Xingu come together
and also poet
you are the voice of those with adhesive tape across their mouths
This is no time for literary criticism.
Nor for attacking the gorrillas with surrealistic poems.
And what use are metaphors if slavery is not a metaphor,
if death in the River of the Dead is not a metaphor,
if the Squadron of Death is not?
Now the people weep on the *pau-de-arara.*
But every rooster that crows in the Brazilian night
is now subversive
it crows *"Revolucão"*
and it's subversive, at the end of each night,
like a girl handing out leaflets or posters about Che,
each red dawn.

Greetings to the farmers, the peons, the laypeople in the jungle,
to the *tapirapé* chief, the Little Sisters of Foucauld, Chico, and
    Rosa.

With a hug from

                              ERNESTO CARDENAL

                    —Translated by Donald D. Walsh

NOTES

1. Solentiname was Cardenal's community in Nicaragua. See *The Gospel in Solentiname,* four volumes published by Orbis Books.
2. DEOPS: *Departamento Estadual de Orden Politica e Social*, Department of Political and Social Order, Brazil's secret police.
3. *Igarapé:* A waterway in the forest passable by canoe; bayou.
4. *Pau-de-arara:* "parrot-perch," a device for torture.

A view of São Félix on the river Araguaia. In the right forefront is the cathedral and to its left is the residence of the bishop and the pastoral team that works in São Félix and the surrounding area. All the facilities are shared with the bishop in this small residence. Visitors are always welcomed. Behind the house is a poultry yard with its chickens and ducks. All this helps to provide eggs and meat for the table which is commonly shared by the pastoral team and the bishop.

Foreword to the English Translation

I am writing this preface to the English-language edition from the same Mato Grosso where I originally held my dialogues with Pedro Casaldáliga. I have come back to visit Pedro, the bishop of this backwoods area, and I am spending a week with him (August 21–28, 1980).

Suffocating in the final intense heat of the drought—five months without a drop of rain—we raise our hands high to welcome the first rainfall as it washes the dust of the road off us. São Félix, Canabrava, Port Alegre, Luciara. . . .

Once again there is the backlands, now wrapped in dense smoke from the fires used to burn the fields before the rains come to reinvigorate the pastures. Once again there is the immense Araguaia, calm and refreshing, maternal, brimming with life under the surface, along the shore, and in the air above. Birds, fish, turtles, and alligators can be seen plainly.

Once again there is Matos, the expert boatman. His son overcame his leprosy and has become a man. There is Sister Irene ("Auntie"), Inés, Father Antonio, Pontín with his wife and children, Tadeu, Sister Magdalena, Judit, Jesús, Manuel (with arthrosis resulting from a fall from a horse), Silvia and Sergio. Once again I meet the members of the São Felix pastoral team, who are struggling in their territory for the Kingdom of God and human beings.

Once again I see the peasants, the poor and perpetually insecure landholders who are now more consciously aware and organized. Once again there are the Indians, merged into one with the river, the beaches, and the woods. They are continually threatened by the greed that rapes their forests, by the saws that topple their trees and frighten away their game, and by the roads that cut through their villages.

And once again there is Pedro—with less flesh and more bone showing, with the same fire and soul, with his hugs and his words. Endless dialogues through the night with Pedro, Manuel, and Isidro. For Isidro it is his first shocked encounter with this region of poverty, injustice, and evangelical accents. All of us sit and talk, enveloped in the festive music of Luciara with its distinctive rhythms and the full glow of the moon.

This English-language edition of my book has benefited from our fresh meeting with Pedro in his Mato Grosso. For its final postscript records our 1980 dialogue with Pedro. Moreover, I feel that the dialogues in this book as a whole retain all of their bloody relevance. Amid some advances and retreats, the basic drama and its problems remain the same. Let me tick them off, chapter by chapter:

1. The repressive military dictatorship, whose last president in Brazil was Geisel, has given way to the "opening up" of President Figueiredo, as demanded by the people and the most clear-sighted groups. Their irreversible awakening was what I described in the first chapter of this book.

Pedro's popularity has become an integral part of the ongoing march of the people's movement, which has grown in force and organization. The old danger of expulsion has disappeared, but the expulsion of foreigners (including missionaries) returns to haunt the future. A new law may open up the old conflict between church and state for the *n*th time.

Frank, peaceable opening-up is not the whole story. The patterns of repression do not automatically fall apart. The terrorism of rightist groups, who oppose the new policy with bombs, has exploded on the scene. Fifteen years of military dictatorship will cost Brazil dearly. The economic crisis has turned into a disaster. The "miracle" is indeed total: the total ruin of a truly rich country, which has been surrendered to foreign imperial masters and wealthy nationals serving as intermediaries. The latter have been converted to the thinking and ways of the foreign masters. Inflation and the foreign debt have gotten beyond all bounds. Gold-fever is the necessary result, as the government looks to that commodity to pay off its debts.

2. Archbishop Sigaud has dropped out of the picture and shut up. But his loud accusations of "communism" against Pedro Casaldáliga, Tomás Balduíno, the Dominicans, and the base-level ecclesial communities (CEBs) are something more than a ridiculous tale. For right now official voices in the senate are directing those same accusations of "communism" against Cardinal Arns, Archbishop Cámara, and Bishop Casaldáliga.

The Vatican silently buried in its archives the results of its investigation concerning Sigaud's accusations. Meanwhile the writings of Pedro Casaldáliga have gone into a fourth edition and are circulating freely in Brazil.

3. Savage capitalism remains the enemy, and land the "number-one problem." The landholders, small peasants, and Indians are the victims. I witnessed the death-threats issued by the capitalist estate against the Christian leader of the Canabrava peasants' union, whose name is Cantidio. The threats came from a hired gunman and a favored bigshot. The enemy continues to be multinational capitalism—imperialist, colonialist, devastating.

4. The immense Araguaia continues to be the great companion, friend, brother, sister, and mother. From its womb flow the waters of life and of death. On its shore I have seen the people of Luciara resurrected during the feasts of their patron saints; and I have seen their "remnant" celebrating the Resurrection with Bishop Pedro. In any case the moving dialogue I had with Pedro

about the nearness of death retains all of its vitality and seriousness, even as Pedro himself retains all his passion for what has
happened: the death being endured by his people; and the death
of his fellow bishop, Oscar Arnulfo Romero, the Latin American
martyr assassinated in San Salvador. Pedro's poem to Romero is
included in the postcript to this English-language edition.

5. The Indians have grown in unity and strength from the realization that they are the last among the last. Without ceasing to be
"the one who must die," the Indian has come to be the one who is
fighting to survive. But besides claiming their rights, the Indians
have, alas, become people who kill as well as get killed. The
fault must be placed on INCRA, which failed to mark out the
boundaries of Indian land. It let the big landowners walk in and
throw out their day-laborers, pushing them toward Indian territory and destruction. Right now, for example, eleven such dis-
placed laborers have been killed by Indians on the Xingú Reservation in Mato Grosso. Elsewhere at least twelve others have been
killed for invading Indian land. It is always the innocent who pay
the price: poor farm workers who do not even realize that they are
destroying the forests and farmlands of the Indians. Meanwhile
the great expropriators and usurpers live peacefully far from
danger, blaming the government and INCRA.

In the new dialogue, that concludes this English-language edition, Pedro talks in Chapter 6 about gains and losses since we met.
He talks about new features in the Brazilian church and that of
São Félix. And he adds remarks about his own personal concerns,
which were discussed in Chapters 7, 8, and 9. A few new poems
are also added.

So I offer my English-language readers all of my dialogues with
Pedro Casaldáliga in Mato Grosso. I greet them as friends. I invite them to ponder the relationship maintained between the rul-
ing powers in their world and the dominated people of the Third
World, the impoverished peasants, day laborers, and Indians: our
condemned brothers and sisters.

Introduction

My earlier volume of dialogues[1] consisted of interviews with European and Latin American theologians, all known and admired by me, and some of them esteemed with a certain personal friendship. The present volume, consisting of dialogues with the bishop of São Félix do Araguaia, however, really goes far beyond the interview genre, for the simple reason that, for me, to have a dialogue with Pedro Casaldáliga is to share his faith, his struggle, his hope—his whole world. I spent a fortnight with him in the beautiful and cruel land of Mato Grosso, and these dialogues are the story of our encounter. The leading roles are played by Pedro himself, his milieu (his people, his struggles, the latest attacks by the forces in power), and his word.

Friendship and journalism have joined here to communicate what friendship usually conceals and what a journalist does not get to see in a celebrity whom he approaches as a professional.

From the hidden lands of Mato Grosso, through which extends the prelature of São Félix, 58,000 square miles of backlands unknown for centuries, the Catalan missionary Bishop Pedro Casaldáliga has become well known in recent years because of his cries of denunciation and his writings. He has made known to Brazil and to the world the brutal sacrifice of entire populations of small farmers, landworkers, and Indians at the hands of the insatiable powers in control of the land.

1

Much earlier, more than twenty-five years ago, I was a close friend of Pedro. I had entered the novitiate that the Claretian missionaries had in Vich, and Pedro was ordained a priest in Barcelona in the same Claretian congregation. In 1952, during my years of seminary training, the name of Casaldáliga, his writings, his radio scripts, his activities with the young and the underprivileged, and his contacts with us were provocative reference points for our apostolic aspirations. When I finished my studies in 1963, Pedro, recently named publisher of our Marian publication *Iris* (which he called "a journal of testimony and hope"), called me to Madrid to be editor-in-chief. We were by then comrades, brothers, friends in the small struggles that the gospel demanded of us in the life and work of that time. In 1968, when Pedro suddenly left for Brazil, a part of me left with him, and there, in uninterrupted communion, that part of me has lived and grown. . . .

That is why I said that for me to have a dialogue with Pedro is to *share.*

In 1973, São Félix was invaded by the military in a terrorist-like attack against the staff and the person of Bishop Casaldáliga. The episcopal vicar, Fr. Leopoldo Belmonte, Fr. Antônio Canuto, and Fr. Pedro Mari Sola were beaten; several young lay members of the pastoral staff were arrested, jailed, and tortured. I wrote an account of those events and an analysis of the situation that spawned them.[2] It was a study documented from the files of letters and pastoral writings of the bishop.

The present volume, however, is based on Pedro himself, his person, his word. Also some of the villages of his prelature, the members of his staff, all his people. And the Araguaia River, the glades, the forest, the skies, the land—the landed estates and their lethal greed.

To talk with Bishop Casaldáliga is to talk with that whole world of his that surrounds him and lives in him, with all that cries out in his word. And with the world and the church of Brazil, and that whole Latin American world and church that he loves passionately.

To talk with Pedro is also—perhaps especially—to bring to the dialogue his poetry. "If I am anything at all," he said to me, "I'm a poet." And it is true. It is in his verses that his whole world becomes in him—eloquently—announcement, testimony, shout, outcry. Poetry and prophecy are his word—his faith, his struggle, his hope. All the verses that embellish my narrative are from his writings. They accompanied me, revealing to me the mysteries of the Mato Grosso, its beauty and its pain, its song and its sorrow. If you ask me the reason for making his dialogue of friendship public, it is because I no longer find any reason to talk with Pedro in privacy. Because he and his world, his problems, his struggle and his word, have become everyone's concern. And not just through publicity but through communion and common responsibility. After all, what is at stake in Mato Grosso, in São Félix, in Bishop Casaldáliga, and in his church and his people, is what is at stake in every square foot of our earth surrounded by barbed wire, bought and sold and stolen by greed and inequitable speculation, drenched with blood. It is what is at stake in every person arrested, tortured, "eliminated." It is what is at stake in our own lands and among our own people. It concerns us all. Pedro Casaldáliga and his people are living, suffering, struggling under great obstacles for what is, in a more or less covert way, our own drama.

I have reasons for opening to everyone my dialogues with Pedro. I am only the witness of a witness. I obey the mandate of Jesus of Nazareth: "Shout from the rooftops what they whisper in your ear." And I warn you that Pedro Casaldáliga is no longer silent about anything. Three years ago, in the prologue to his book *¡Yo creo en la justicia y en la esperanza!* [I Believe in Justice and Hope!],[3] I said that faith and audacity (the boldness of his hope) had done away with his old inhibitions, had set him free to talk open-heartedly. I told him that it would bring him grave troubles, even within the church, because through the centuries we have lost in the church the freedom to speak according to the gospel. I told him that there would be some who would rend their garments and turn him over to inquisition. And that is what happened. (And it will happen again, because of the logic hardened into the systems, both inside and outside the church, that react to public accusations.) The powers have repeatedly tried to expel Bishop Casaldáliga from Brazil. Archconservative ecclesiastical circles have vociferously accused him of being "communist and subversive" and have asked the Vatican and the military government to remove him. And the Vatican appointed a papal legate to investigate the accusations.

That is another, urgent reason, to publish these dialogues with Pedro. I reached him at just the moment when all the powers were allied against him and his cause, his person and his church. This cause, the common cause of humanity and the gospel, is always under attack, but there are always a few who will struggle prophetically against the common enemy. I found Pedro under attack by calumny and conspiracy, and it is my duty to cry out the truth to the four winds. For our common cause, I cry out what I have seen, what I have heard, what I have read.

Maybe the time has come to break silence about everything. The day may come (it certainly will come) when we shall be left only with the word, nothing more (and nothing less) than the word, and we must stake our lives on it, for the dignity of all, for freedom and for life.

When I said goodbye to Pedro, on the bank of the immense Araguaia, near the Santa Terezinha jail, a mute witness to the pain and the fire (mute also the roosters that filled my nights with crowing, in the *sertão*, the backlands of Mato Grosso), I said to him: "If our dialogues inspire some verses in you, write them down and send them to me. I'll put them in the introduction to the book." Pedro laughed; he said only: "We'll see." I had wrung him dry in those two weeks. I had abused the gift of his word, which is one of his charisms. (He had once expressed the poetic-prophetic desire to have himself baptized again by his mother, "with the water of sobs," when he discovered in grief what freedom was, and he asked for himself the name "Pedro-Freedom," *Pedro-Libertad*; but I elaborated on that theme and gave him the name "Pedro-Freedom-of-Speech," *Pedro Libertad de Palabra*.) And, knowing that what was impossible he would find a way to make possible, I waited for those verses. And now that the book has been put together, just as I am finishing the introduction, from an unexpected source his verses reach me. I present them here. They are "circumstantial" verses, framing our dialogues and providing the key for reading them as we lived them—in the Mato Grosso.

These Raucous Roosters Answer You

You ask me about my faith

(while little Ana-Elisa laughs,
as remote, as beloved, as secure
as Lozano's angel who ate tender roses;

while I put wood on the fire,
stirring up my resolve,
by the love of a papaya the size of a throb;

while you read, frightened, the Passion according to Frei Tito;

while the stylized cock cries out
my decrepit, impenitent identity;

while the lamp of anxiety
fills with accustomed penumbra
this fleeting and unstructured cathedral;

while the Araguaia comes, like a sea within reach;
while the seagulls, *in memoriam*, cut out like pages thrown into
the wind,
fly over the seashore and my forehead:
friends, places, moments, projects, griefs;

while the River of Present Death flows along freely;

while the ever-present
sun sets
as absolute
as God;

while, with the evening, comes hope).

I answer you with my life.
With the life of my world without justice and without voice.

With the life of your world without justice and without ears.
With the earth still perfumed by its breath.
With the earth blackened into huge estates.
With my tongue babbling again, always a child.
With men who harbor me, who harbor you, for my cause,
for their cause.
With the poor of the land without land.
With the dead ambushed by the living.
With the streets without signs, without bricks, without keys.
With houses and bellies bursting with infants.
With the cows that cross our path, heads lowered, coming back,
    their eyes dotted with a thousand specks and their lyre-horns
    submissive.

You ask me so many important things
    (important for a book with censure;
      for suitable words from the mouth of a bishop, in the odor of
        magisterium;
      for long vistas, between myth and enchiridion).

Put your ear in tune with the neighboring birds,
with the nearby galaxies.
Brother, if you can, tell
in tonight's codes,
the extent of the promise.
Take note with your soul. Don't insist on recording me.
Don't magnetically can my bitterness and my joy.
Don't put my questions as answers.
Don't let it seem that I define the indefinable hope.
Don't put a binding on so many pages, so many wings, so many
    winds,
so many angers, so many deaths, so much grace . . .

You ask me so many ineffable things.
I know only that I don't know much of what I used to know
    before (by rote, by decree).
I know only that I'm freer,
learning to play the man playing the Indian.
I ratify, in any case, that I certainly want to go on being a poet.

Living for utopia (which we call gospel),
Dying full of hope.

You ask about my faith.
Shall I give you a simple answer?
 I believe in God.
 I believe in people.
 I believe in the Lord Jesus.
 I believe in poor Mary and in the whole poor church.
 I believe in everybody's earth, like the first mother.
 I believe in new places,
     with a place for laughing out of doors
        (nature again);
     with a place to feel that you're company
        (humanity again);
     with a place to live eternal life
        (now in time);
     with a place to wait for eternal glory.

Shall I answer you by asking impertinently?
 Your Jalón and my Araguaia,
    are they two rivers?
 Your Madrid and my *Sertão*,
    are they two places?
 Your Europe and our America,
    are they one world?
 Our canon, arranged each day,
    is it the *stricte talis*[4] mass?
 Our Bible, decanted into *cauí tapirapé*,[5]
    does it have its *nihil obstat*[6] for your palates?
 You're our other church,
    is it now *the* church?
 The living God of these poor people,
    is he ours, oh Teófilo?

These roosters that persist, into the night, shrill clarion calls,
piercing the darkness, challenging the stars and the stock
  markets;
rigid sentinels, braced against sleep, as often as is needed;

these roosters born and alive and always on duty
so that nobody will sleep, foreign to the testimony,
if he did not previously make his alliance
with the night and with the dawn.

These roosters (that crow to us) are the roosters of the guilt of
Saint Peter.
These roosters (that call to us) are the roosters of Mary's vigil,
These roosters (that sing to us) are the roosters of the sepulcher,
mane prima sabbati!!![7]

Are there no longer any roosters in Europe,
that you should be amazed at these roosters?

You ask me about my faith.
They answer you with questions, our raucous roosters!

PEDRO CASALDÁLIGA
Bishop of São Félix do Araguaia
Mato Grosso

With grateful love to Pedro and his people, with hope for
everyone, for the cause of humanity and the gospel, I present the
pages that follow.

TEOFILO CABESTRERO

Teofilo Cabestrero (right) with Bishop Casaldáliga: "For my friends over there, you are my letter and my message. Give them all that we have and are, and what we are hoping for."

"For us Pedro is a brother, a father, a friend, a person who enlightens us, who shows us the way of God's life, teaches us to struggle together with a people mistreated and persecuted. Pedro gives us the example of life, he gives courage."

1

Too Popular to Be Exiled

Brazil Is a Volcano

The students have moved freely from their campuses to the streets, the journalists and publishers have acquired a great freedom of expression, and the legalized political opposition has tried to stop being an ornamental opposition. Publicly they call for "democratic freedoms," "amnesty for political prisoners," "an end to the torturing," "immediate release of prisoners and jailed students," "the end of repressive dictatorship.". . .

A Brazilian assures me that the government has let things get out of hand, the economy is weak, serious corruption is being discovered, and the system is falling apart everywhere. "But nobody knows whether we are moving toward change and flexibility, or, on the contrary, the government will enforce even harsher repression."

The Latin American giant is waking abruptly from the dream of the "Brazilian miracle." It sees that its foreign debt has increased. It discovers that the great masses of the people have become more impoverished while the powerful classes have increased their wealth. It sees that its working class is paid very low wages—cheap labor for the profits of the multinational corporations. It sees that the small farmers of its extensive rural regions are left landless despite immense, uncultivated land holdings—the preserves of the huge companies that soak up governmental funding. All this existed before, but now it is seen and publicly denounced.

Events collide and contradict one another, creating uncertainty. Examples: Brazil has a parliament (unique among the military regimes in Latin America), but the president, General Geisel, dissolved it for two months in 1978, the easier to impose his decrees. One night in June, José de Alencar Furtado, leader of the Brazilian Democratic Movement (MDB, *Movimento Democrático Brasilero*), the only opposition party legally permitted but also legally muzzled, criticized the government on television with such unaccustomed freedom that Brazilians were amazed (a curious law grants two hours a year on television to the legal opposition); but two days later President Geisel suspended the mandate and the political rights of the unfortunate leader of the MDB. Faced with such authoritarianism, the MDB is considering dissolving itself in order to expose the farce of Brazilian parliamentarism.

People talk and write with astonishing naturalness about returning to democracy and to a state of law, about returning power to civilians and sending the military back to their barracks. There is a segment of the military that desires this too, in opposition to the hard-liners. The opposition party proposes freedom without revenge. "We must not seek revenge for the tortures of the last thirteen years," says Pedro Simón, one of the directors of the MDB, "nor send to prison the leaders, ex-presidents and other persons. It must all be forgotten." They even point to the figure of

Magalhaes Pinto, the astute independent banker, as a key element in "national pacification." But the Death Squadron has again sown terror in the streets after two years of silence. Sixty deaths in one month is quite a record.

No one knows if it is a matter of members of the Mafia and other criminals settling accounts between themselves, or of once more silencing outbursts of freedom. The fact is that the archbishop of Rio de Janeiro, Dom Eugenio Sales, who had been on good terms with the regime until the brutal abduction of neighborhing Bishop Hypólito Adriano (an abduction that has gone unpunished) and the regime's support of divorce, denounced the Death Squadron in a broadcast in which he suggested that the Squadron's members were themselves policemen.

Much to my surprise, Brazil is now a volcano of chain explosions, a tidal wave of pent-up waters about to burst in fury. Beneath the apparent calm of repression a ferment of freedom has been quietly growing, like the growth of an unrestrainable jungle. And new outcries are being heard, protected now by the proclamations of the new policy of the United States that promotes the "defense of human rights." After feeding repression for fifteen years, first in Brazil and then in Uruguay, Bolivia, Chile, and Argentina, perhaps goaded by a guilty conscience and certainly in order to cleanse its public image, the United States is now asking that human rights be respected in Latin America—a slogan masking a tactic that can deceive only the naive, but that could produce uncontrollable results in Brazil.

Bishop Pedro Casaldáliga, wagering on hope, has written of this awakening: "One day freedom will also dawn on this new homeland, green and gold, which has definitively become itself."

In this convulsed Brazil, the church is an ancient voice, a friend of the poor and oppressed, tempered in the fire of persecution and martyrdom, comrade of the people. Repression preyed upon the church from the time when, with the establishment of the present military regime in 1964, the church was the only pocket of freedom, the only voice for a silenced people. Arrests, tortures, expulsions, and assassinations have tried to stiffle that free voice. There was the murder of Father Pereira, secretary of Dom Hélder Câmara, dead after undergoing terrible torture in 1968; the slanders and the brutal torture of the Dominicans arrested in 1969; the harassment of the militant lay persons of the dioceses of Volta Redonda and Cratéus, whose bishops, Waldyr Calheiros and Antônio Fragoso, are, with Hélder Câmara, in the forefront of this prophetic and suffering church of Brazil.

In the years of 1976 and 1977, with the other leaders eliminated, there was increased persecution of that church so deeply committed to the people. In Barbatana they tried to kill the bishop of Itapipoca, shooting at him while he was preaching a sermon. They kidnapped the bishop of Nova Iguaçu, Dom Hypólito Adriano; they insulted him, stripped him, painted his whole body red, beat him, and left him naked in the middle of the night; they left his overturned car in front of the building housing the Episcopal Conference in Rio de Janeiro. They killed Father Rodolfo Lunkenbein and the Indian Simão of the Bororo Indian mission in Meruri. A policeman murdered Father João Bosco, with a point-blank shot to the head, with an explosive bullet, in Ribeirão Bonito, Mato Grosso. They arrested and tortured Father Florentino Maboni in Pará. They arrested, harassed, and exiled Father Giuseppe Fontanella, Vicar of Vila Redonda, in the prelature of Guamá. Father Romain Zufferey, a sixty-six-year-old Swiss, chaplain of the Catholic Workers Association, had his office in Recife broken into several times and was expelled by provisions of the law of national security. They arrested the missionaries Thomas Capuano, a Protestant, and Lawrens Resebaugh, an Oblate of Mary Immaculate; both were mistreated in Recife, where their work with the poor was considered "subversion" (Capuano was expelled from the country after being refused a renewal of his permit to stay in Brazil). They have orchestrated to the full the accusations of the rightist defender of the regime, Archbishop Geraldo Proença Sigaud, against the bishops of Goiás and São Félix, Thomás Balduino and Pedro Casaldáliga, charging them with being communists because of their pastoral support of farm workers and Indians, and demanding that Bishop Casaldáliga be expelled from Brazil. The Dominican Order, eighty other bishops, and all the church-related grassroots communities (*comunidades de base*) should be suspected of "communism and subversion"— according to Archbishop Sigaud's statement. Two other bishops, Dom Estevão of Conceição do Aragia and Dom Alano of Marabá, were subjected to interrogation by the military; they were accused of "armed violence" for supporting the tenants dispossessed of their lands who defended themselves against their invaders, the forces of the landowners. Several bishops state that they and their dioceses are the outright object of outright espionage: there are investigations into their ideas, their funds, and possible personal vices. There have been several cases of blackmail. It has been discovered that agents of the International Information Service (SNI, *Serviço Internacional de Informação*—the Brazilian counterpart to the North American CIA) have infiltrated seminaries.

To learn all this in a few days, on arriving in Brazil, is quite a shock. My head is spinning as we fly from São Paulo to Brasilia, graciously served by the Varig flight attendants.

As we descend for the landing, I see that red earth inundated with green and dotted with flowering trees. Everything is burning in an immense setting sun.

Brazil is a volcano.

A Bishop Who Is Too Popular

I cannot help seeing on the crest of the wave of this angry sea the "insignificant" bishop of the remote prelature of São Félix, as popular here as a banner of freedom. I have been stunned to see this dear "soul mate," this good friend and brother, Pedro Casaldáliga, applauded by some, denigrated by others.

"He's too popular now to be banished," they tell me. And "well informed sources" state that the plan for his expulsion, on the point of being carried out, was aborted *in extremis* because of the pressure of the bishops and the outcry of public opinion. I know very well that Pedro has always felt attracted by silence, called by the desert, because of his "instinct for solitude."

Tiny, remote São Félix, hidden among rivers and woods, now suffers an invasion of journalists—American, German, English, French, Spanish, and even Brazilian—and some television crews. First the show staged by the accusations of Dom Sigaud (on TV-Globo, prime time, in the national press, and even in faked diocesan bulletins), the debates of senators and deputies, the well reasoned and courageous answers of Pedro; next, his bold accusations before the Parliamentary Land Commission, in full public view; and now the risk of imminent explusion and the personal investigation of the Vatican legate, have all resulted in making him tremendously popular throughout the country, this bishop who lives between the most unjust accusations and threats and the most clamorous support. His name has been acclaimed by students in demonstrations and vibrantly applauded by the five thousand participants in the homage to Cardinal Paulo Evaristo Arns, archbishop of São Paulo, because of his repeated defense of human fights. Just at the time of his deepest trouble (accusations, possible explusion, Vatican investigation), Bishop Casaldáliga was elected by the Law School of São Paulo to the post of "Defender of Human Rights," an honor granted on the occasion of the 150th anniversary of the institution's foundation.

I am curious to know how Pedro reacts to so much popularity. I ask him: "They've praised you to the sky and put you in the pillory. How does this leave you? What does this mean to you? How do you feel?"

Pedro, who is very intuitive, answers quickly: "Well, look, I think that, like everyone, I'm vain, and it might perhaps have pleased me to be praised. Fortunately, in the midst of all this there are two serious circumstances that prevent me from yielding much to vanity. I don't say that I haven't had my faults, but I couldn't give way to vanity thanks to these circumstances. First, the responsibility for, the needs of, this little church that, like it or not, I feel weighing me down at all times, and this prevents me, of course, from playing the fool. The second circumstance is the presence of death."

Pedro looked at me. It was nighttime. By the pale light I saw the look in his tired eyes (he has had a cataract operation on one eye, and his other eye is sentenced to the same operation). I assure you that he is sincere when he mentions death.

"The presence of death has helped me greatly to feel myself in the presence of the Lord, who is the only judge when the time of reckoning arrives. I remember having read in my student years that death gives specific weight to life. It does, doesn't it? That closeness of death makes one more serious and sharpens one's responsibility: you see, it's not a question of pretending or lying, it's not a question of selling goods, not a question of writing literature; it's a question of the church, it's a question of the people who are there, in the tragedy. And we live the tragedy here so concretely, so rudely, that at times you feel like disappearing in search of calm, like retreating to a desert. But I've never liked to flee from community responsibilities. I've felt this from childhood, since I was a boy. By temperament, by training, and by grace, I have decided to stay in the tragedy."

Pedro pauses, and I can sense the night. The night is warm and clear. The moon is full. There are very few pauses in Pedro's speech. He talks fast, almost impetuously ("my mother's way of talking: easy, nervous, incisive"). His Spanish is very fluent for someone who has been talking Portuguese in Brazil for ten years, even though a few Portuguese phrases escape from him. "I always talk in Portuguese, at times I think, pray, and sing in Catalan, and I have to go on writing in Spanish." Pedro still has his resonant voice, strong but whispery, all lungs and soul. Now he speaks to me in the soft tone of confidence.

"Fortunately we work as a team and we always think as a team, with the help of theologians and pastoralists, and in dialogue with other churches. For some years now we've been feeling a kind of popularity, those repercussions because of our lives and our activities. We've examined this several times, thinking of its pros and cons, and we've concluded that we bear responsibility also to what lies beyond the frontiers of the prelature. We often do more outside than inside; what we are and what we do inside here has more repercussions outside. And they've also told us this in meetings and in letters. So whether it's the pillory or the pedestal, we've accepted it with a certain simplicity, with a certain responsibility, with a spirit of collegiality in the best sense of the word, which is that of 'communion.' And it hasn't become torture, anguish. No. Although it has left me—I won't say sleepless, because you know that I sleep; when the time comes, I sleep soundly—but it *has* left me worried, deeply worried. Do you know what happens? To the extent that you receive responsibility and reverses, you also receive affection, communion, and support. So there's a compensating balance."

We had not seen each other for ten years. When I arrived in Brazil I found that Pedro was in Goiás, on a short retreat from his Mato Grosso, and I came to seek him out on this side of the Araguaia, between the river and Brasilia. The immense Araguaia is the boundary between the states of Goiás and Mato Grosso, between the diocese of Dom Tomás Balduino and Pedro's prelature, the two bishops of the two most persecuted churches in Brazil at this time. "Brother Araguaia" unites them in a single current of ideas and commitments, in the face of the conflicts with the great landed estates (*latifundios*), of the development and power of capitalism directed against the farmers, the workers, and the Indians.

On a bus, my eyes stunned by the landscape that burns under a merciless sun (the silent green hills, the tall trees of all colors, the meadows, the cattle), I have come to this noble city of Goiás Velho with its cobbled streets, where the green harmonizes with the old stones and where they charge you almost fifty cents for a photocopy (five times more than in São Paulo: how and why does speculation grow?).

Ten years without seeing each other, but I feel that our arms, our chests, our backs recognize each other as if they had lived in an *abrazo*. We talk. We talk greedily, endlessly, heedless of the hour. We talk of everybody and of everything, when we're working and when we're eating ("with these fruits and vegetables my liver is better"; Pedro maintains his precarious health despite the threats of malaria and hepatitis). And we talk at ease, wrapped in the cordiality of the good people who make livable this great center for the training of leaders, this forge of Christian strength of this church of Dom Tomás and his collaborators.

I tell Pedro that I have come with a head whirling from all that I have seen, heard, and read in these few days.

"I've been told that they don't expel you because you're too popular. Do you think that is important to the Brazilian government?"

"That's what I've often wondered. I've often said to myself, I've even commented on it with the group, that the government thinks we are much more than we really are, that they view us as—I don't know what. I'm convinced that if the president had just added the signature needed to expel me, there would have been an uproar for two, three, four days, a week or two. . . . And then what? So many things have happened!"

His imagination conjures up the sequel: "I would arrive in beloved Old Spain and there you would all give me testimonials, dinners, fervent masses. . . . And a book or two would be published. . . . So what? . . . Don't you think so?"

His humor is contagious. We joke, we laugh. Then he takes off his glasses. I notice more clearly the weariness in his eyes.

"Well, now, talking seriously: they have certainly thought that I am the church, that I am the bishop, that I am—in quotes—the Vatican. And they have also thought that I am public opinion, national and international. Besides, you know that in Brazil the government finds itself more and more in an internal struggle between the hardest possible line and a more liberal line. Its strength isn't consolidated enough that it can allow itself the luxury of struggle with 'the church,' which is the 'other' power (and we'll have to talk about that). It seems to me that that has its influence."

The Impossible Expulsion

"The latest news is again the rumor of my expulsion. They say that now he's going. It's possible." Pedro doesn't know whether to give credence to such things, in spite of the fact that he knows that the president's signature was about to be put on the decree of expulsion. "At any rate," he adds, "God is God, as the people say, and nobody is expelling God. And each new injustice by 'them' (the big ones) is a new victory for 'these' (the little ones)."

The "latest news" broke out on July 30 at 3 P.M. with a statement to the press of Rio de Janeiro by the secretary of the Episcopal Conference, Dom Ivo Lorscheiter: "Reliable sources in Brasilia and Goiânia have warned us that the expulsion of Dom Pedro Casaldáliga from Brazil is imminent." Nobody could imagine such a thing, with the ashes of the fiery accusations of Dom Sigaud cold and almost forgotten in Brazil. It had the appearance of a lightning attack. The press itself emphasized that in the government palaces and in the nunciature in Brasilia there was neither confirmation nor denial of Dom Ivo's alarming declaration, which continued: "We insistently appeal to the responsible organs of the government that such an act of injustice and hostility to the church not take place."

"Reliable sources." Who alerted the bishops? Who let them know that the decree of expulsion of the bishop of São Félix was ready and waiting on the president's desk? A week earlier, the Rio edition of the newspaper *O Estado de São Paulo* and the Rio office of the international "France Presse" agency received anonymous telephone calls announcing that the expulsion of Bishop Casaldáliga was only a "question of days." Nobody took this announcement seriously; it wasn't even noticed by the bishops. It is thought that the notice came from somewhere high in government circles, from sources very close to the high command that started the chain of events. Of course, there are also high *military* figures "explicitly" in favor of denunciation and expulsion of the controversial bishop of São Félix.

The alarm spread rapidly. To its thirteen regional secretariats came the notice of the National Conference of the Brazilian Bishops (CNBB, *Conferência Nacional dos Bispos do Brasil*) about the rumored expulsion of the Spanish bishop. Within hours, telegrams of protest began raining down on the highest government offices.

The press kept track of the presiding bishops of the regional conferences who made critical statements and of those who kept silence. Nine of the thirteen presiding bishops sent their express protests. "There is no reason to be surprised by the silence of the four other regional conferences if one takes into account the characteristics of the bishops who preside over them." The archbishop of Porto Alegre, Dom Vicente Scherer, who presides over the Third Southern Region (Río Grande del Sur), is one of the three or four most conservative bishops in Brazil. He could be one of the few supporters of the accusations of Dom Sigaud against Casaldáliga. The other three, the primate, Dom Avelar Brandão, the archbishop of Rio de Janeiro, Dom Eugenio de Araújo Sales, and Dom João de Souza Lima, archbishop of Manaus, are described as "among the more moderate members of the episcopacy."

The episcopal commentaries emphasize that the expulsion of a bishop has no precedent in Brazil, that the confrontation between the government and the church would be blunt and "the reactions unforeseeable." It would lead to a "very delicate" situation in a Brazil where, of the 218 ecclesiastical subdivisions, 42 are prelatures (like that of São Félix) which cover more than half of the national territory, and 33 of which are administered by foreign bishops: Italians, Spaniards, Germans, Austrians, Dutch, Americans, and Canadians.

The seriousness of the act and the affection felt for the person and the pastoral work of Bishop Casaldáliga provoked strong protests addressed to President Geisel. "We express the disapproval of this episcopate and of the people of God. The measure, highly offensive and unjust, wounds Christian feelings and signifies an attitude diametrically opposed to the church in Brazil" (Dom Fernando Gomes, archbishop of Goiânia). "The bishops of the State of São Paulo reemphasize their total solidarity with Dom Pedro Casaldáliga; we do not entertain even the possibility that the government expel a bishop so devoted to the poor. This would violently wound the Christian and Catholic feelings of our people" (Cardinal Paulo Evaristo Arns, archbishop of São Paulo). Dom Hélder Câmara: "If the expulsion takes place, it will be a serious act of injustice and hostility directed against the Catholic Church." "We protest the expulsion, in the name of the gospel and the Declaration of Human Rights" (Dom Pedro Defalto, archbishop of Curitiba). The Justice and Peace Commission issued a communiqué in São Paulo to "manifest publicly its deep consternation at the flagrant injustice of any decision that would oblige the bishop of São Félix to leave our country, where, in such a markedly evangelical way, even at the risk of his life, he has done so much in favor of the oppressed, the weak, and the persecuted."

The most extensive and most outspoken statement in defense of the work of the threatened bishop was signed by Dom Moacyr Grechi in the name of the bishops' Commission on the Rural Ministry, over which he presides. After recalling the "hundreds" of priests, religious, and lay persons who have suffered unjust arrest, maltreatment, torture, and expulsion, he affirms that this would be the end, that no more can be tolerated, that he and his people denounce the "malevolent intent" to "wound the shepherd in order to disperse the flock." He noted that the pope himself said to the cardinal of São Paulo in 1976, when there was also talk of expelling Dom Pedro Casaldáliga: "To touch the bishop of São Félix is to touch the pope." And he concluded: "We do not accept the continuation of this insidious campaign against Dom Pedro Casaldáliga. We reject even the *talk* of driving him out of the country. His exemplary pastoral work in the prelature of São Félix do Araguaia must continue. The farmers and the Indians of that tragic area of the Amazon, whom their bishop has been defending with evangelical courage for ten years; the farmers, Indians, and workers throughout Brazil, who are finding in the church relief from their suffering in the hope of the Christian message of freedom; the whole Brazilian people, who see in the church's commitment to the poor and persecuted the concrete and effective translation of the gospel of Jesus for our reality; and finally the church, Brazilian and universal, which refuses to see repeated in Brazil a violent interference with its work, an interference that occurs only where the persecution of Christians is the official policy—all of these require the presence of Dom Pedro in Brazil."

The Vatican nuncio in Brazil, Dom Carmine Rocco, questioned by jounalists in Brasilia about the expulsion of Bishop Casaldáliga, said: "It's an endemic case, because it comes up periodically. But I don't believe it will occur, although I don't say that it can't occur under any circumstances."

"God grant that this never happen," the people said through the mouth of Giselda. "Because for us Pedro is a brother, a father, a friend, a person who enlightens us, who shows us the way of God's life, teaches us to struggle together with a people mistreated and persecuted. Pedro gives us the example of life, he gives us courage. He is never discouraged, and without him things here would be much more difficult."

It does not happen this time. The firmness of the bishops, the seriousness of their protests ("the other power"), and the outcry of public opinion stayed the lightning stroke that was going to decree expulsion. An official communiqué from the Ministry of Justice, urgently broadcast on television, assured everyone that there would be no expulsion. Nevertheless, it is thought here that it was the high military command that urged the decree of expulsion, as a counterblow to the bishop's denunciation two weeks earlier before a parliamentary land commission. He had accused three generals of bribing the mayor of Luciara to favor the Codeara landowning company by clearing lands to the harm of the tenants.

The national and international press echoed the bishop's

denunciation of the military. Two days later the high military command issued its public reply defending the honor of the three generals denounced by the bishop. The *secret* reply would be rushed to President Geisel's desk—the decree of expulsion.

Up to now, this has been the closest Pedro Casaldáliga has come to expulsion.

"That's not the problem that worries me most," Pedro said to me very decisively.

"The Problem Is that the People Must Be Able to Live"

"What is it that most concerns me? When persecution gets more violent and there is so much talk of expelling me, when the Holy See names a legate to investigate the accusations that are made against me, what do I expect from the highest spheres of the church, from the Brazilian Bishops' Conference, from the nunciature, from the Vatican, from the pope?

"I would like to expect nothing. I would like to expect what unfortunately certain priests have been able to expect and above all certain lay persons, certain workers, and certain farmers who have been exiled or expelled, tortured, imprisoned, killed, or who disappeared, thrown into the river. At times nothing has been done about it, at times a little document has been written, a little word of support, or a mass has been offered, and that's all. I don't know why a bishop has to be different. I have already written this at a very serious moment. And in the letter that Tomás and I wrote some weeks ago the pope, in connection with the accusations of Dom Sigaud and the use they tried to make of them against our pastoral work, we told him expressly that we are not asking for special attention in any way; that's not the point."

A rest is called for. Pedro has been talking with great intensity.

"Well, now, I must add quite simply that on this point some of my companions in the episcopate and certain other persons have made me do some thinking. They believe that I am responsible to my people, to my little church, and that I am responsible also to the church of Brazil, and that at this crucial hour I can't permit myself the luxury of being held in less esteem. They believe I should demand action from the Brazilian hierarchy, from the

Bishops' Conference, and from the Vatican. Not for *me* but for the cause I represent. Since at times they don't take action as they ought to in the case of a farmer or a laborer, let them at least take action when the victim is a bishop. And this seems to me a positive thing. I must even say, with all respect, that on several occasions I believe that the presidency of the CNBB, the Bishops Conference, was a bit indecisive. On one occasion even, at the time of the Santa Terezinha conflict, there was some ambiguity in the attitude of one of the three elements in the presidency.

"The nunciature has always been sadly diplomatic. You know very well that I am allergic to the diplomacy of the nunciature, and, I believe, with good reason, not just as a personal reaction. It seems to me that it is an excrescence on the body of the church. I don't know how to fit it in, in any of the dogmas, in any of the sacraments, in any of the charisms, in any of the pages of the gospels; there's no place for it, frankly, no room for it. And there have been moments when I seriously believed the nunciature didn't do what it should have done and could have done. If you sound out the opinions of the bishops on this point, you'll see that I'm not the only one who thinks this way about this nunciature."

I have verified that Pedro's "allergy" is not a mania, not a capricious phobia. On the one hand, he has had sad and painful experiences with the nunciature. On the other hand, I have seen very respectable segments of the Brazilian Conference of Bishops clearly reticent about certain actions of the nuncio, Carmine Rocco. And I have read in newspapers this significant statement: "There is renewed talk about transferring the Vatican's representation in this country from the nunciature to the Episcopal Conference." Just gauge the public importance of such an allergy! I have also learned that the pope has been informed recently about actions of the nunciature which have not been in harmony with the bishops and the CNBB. I wrote once that there would be a burst of joy in heaven when the church moves beyond the present system of nunciatures.

In his simple preference for the gospel over diplomacy, Pedro does not fail to see and appreciate the support that he has received at times from the top. He appreciates it all the more when it is evangelical and public support for the cause of Jesus and his good news for the poor, the favorites of the Father.

"Of course, I must now thank the presidency of the CNBB and

all the bishops for their support at this time. I am thankful to Dom Ivo and Dom Aloisio. I must also thank Cardinal Paulo Evaristo of São Paulo for his meetings with and personal communications to the pope at other serious moments. Specifically, in August two years ago, when my expulsion was also being urged, and after waiting some five or six days until the monsignors opened their doors to let him in (him, an archbishop and cardinal), Dom Paulo was able to explain to the pope face to face the situation here, the meaning of our little church. That was when the pope, after praising the missionaries, said that laying a hand on me would mean laying a hand on the pope. I am grateful. I should even be somewhat grateful to the *Osservatore Romano.* You know that I have never been especially fond of the *Osservatore Romano,* for it has seemed to me a newspaper that has stayed up in Michelangelo's dome and has not come down to feel the pulse of the universal church. Of course, it prints the words of the pope, which deserve all my respect and affection, but the paper has always seemed to me a bit constricted, excessively solemn; it does not have any heart nor does it encourage action. So it seems to me. Well, the *Osservatore Romano* printed a rather positive comment on my book *¡Yo creo en la justicia y en la esperanza! (I Believe in Justice and Hope!),* which, of course, coming from the Vatican, in a semiofficial publication of the Holy See, amounted to explicit support by the Vatican. I must be grateful."

Pedro is afraid that he has wandered from the question and he wants to restate his answer in a few words:

"I want the hierarchy, the Vatican, and the whole Brazilian church to understand that the problem is not *mine*—whether or not *I* am expelled. The problem is not Sigaud vs. Casaldáliga. I would like them to see that this is the problem: Vatican II really occurred and must be lived out; Medellín really occurred and must be lived out; and the people really exist and they must be able to live. That is what I would like to have understood. That is what I expect."

The evening is pure twilight. Twilight here is luminous and brief. The sun shimmers a little, and the air becomes transparent and quiet, as if the day suddenly fell silent to welcome the night with serenity. Over the courtyard of this leadership training center now shine the tiny stars of this luminous sky of Goiás.

"I am indeed totally opposed to any dictatorship, capitalist or communist, military or civil. I am against all violence and lack of respect for human rights, whether in Latin America or Siberia."

2

The Archbishop's Anticommunism

Some Repugnant Accusations

"When Dom Sigaud and his colleagues said that now there were not two communist bishops but fifty-one or perhaps eighty, not even fools believed it." Pedro told me this in a tone of relief, as if he felt publicly absolved.

The twenty-three accusations of Archbishop Sigaud against the bishop of São Félix caricature Casaldáliga as a terrorist monster of international communism. They said he deserved the death penalty; his writings deserved a bonfire. The Sigaud document is a crazy quilt of mutilated quotations from the prose and poetry of

Pedro, misunderstood and at times purposely falsified. They try to substantiate slanderous statements broadcast by the archbishop himself some weeks before the appearance of the document.

Reading the Sigaud document calls for a disciplined exercise of almost all the virtues, especially patience and forgiveness; one has to have rigid self-control not to feel indignation, even hatred. An example. Pedro says: "A few days ago I had a discussion with a group of professors and intellectuals who were seeking the reality of freedom in their lives, and were considering the Marxist option as an answer to the problems of contemporary society."[1] Dom Sigaud has him say: "I am seeking a solution, using the Marxist option, as an answer to the problems of contemporary society."

Nevertheless, to make clear in Brazil the exaggeration and the falseness of Dom Sigaud's denunciation of the bishop took five months of polemics and wars of words that monopolized the front pages of the country's newspapers and had strong echoes in the international press. Pedro said to me:"We have lost time gossiping." But this shows the power of the enemy, the influence of ridiculous accusations that no normal person ought to take seriously, and even less the church. It exposes a painful interrelationship of society and church, showing the interplay of the forces and interests that control everything.

The launching of the Sigaud document was crassly spectacular. It was put on by the government-controlled TV-Globo during prime time and published on three whole pages of the leading newspapers. It turned up mysteriously in ordinary households, mailed in printings of faked diocesan bulletins, like the one of the diocese of Nova Iguaçu, known throughout the country as progressive and suffering greatly from repression. "It's an old tactic that they use," Pedro tells me. "They used it against us on another occasion, showing to a national TV audience a bulletin with the masthead of our diocesan bulletin *Alvorada* [Dawn]. The hammer and sickle appeared over an article in favor of Chinese communism. The CIA's strategy against the Latin American church, contained in documents that had come into the hands of the Brazilian bishops, outlined very similar tactics: to plant false evidence for an accusation."

The reaction to the Sigaud document was tumultuous. All the

voices that had been critical of Pedro before were joined against him; others came to his defense. Senators and deputies made their speeches, for or against, and the papers were filled with headlines, speeches, statements, and commentaries about the accused and the accuser. On the same page where Dom Sigaud appeared in all his shining archepiscopal regalia, in a proud and paternal pose, Pedro and Tomás appeared in shirt sleeves, natural, dynamic, simple.

There was soon a shower of articles expressing solidarity with the accused and denunciation of the accuser. Statements from bishops and their clergy, religious, Christian groups, church communities, intellectuals, students, and even some deputies and senators. Only one bishop publicly expressed his support of the accusations of Dom Sigaud, Dom José Pedro Costa, archbishop of Uberaba. Public opinion finally supported the two accused bishops, criticized and even jeered at Dom Sigaud for his demonstrated reactionism and his grave and slanderous hostility against two brother bishops. The press recalled that Archbishop Geraldo Proença Sigaud was one of the founders of "Tradition-Family-Property"(TFP, an acronym that Brazilians sarcastically translate as *Todos Filhos de Puta* [All Sons of a Bitch]). TFP is an ultra-conservative movement that operates in several countries, with a real anticommunist phobia, uses the Fatima devotion to its own ends, and is said to be financed in Brazil by a multinational corporation. The press itself disclosed that Dom Sigaud owned "12,600 acres of land, 100,000 square feet of coffee plantings, 1,000 head of cattle, 30,000 acres planted in eucalyptus trees, with 1,500 workers in his employ." Conflicting accounts have been published on this. One newspaper defended him, saying that the archbishop had created "nearly 35,000 jobs" with his property and plantations. There was also a press report about his activity as president of the rural cooperative of Diamantina, and there were some very significant anecdotes about this. The angriest reactions were insulting, calling him, in print, "big farmer, estate owner, pastor of heifers." The tone of these reactions judged the archbishop very harshly, painting him as a Judas.

There were excesses, of course. The archbishop's zeal cost him some suffering. He had his own press, for the newspapers of the great capitalists and landowners of Brazil always supported Dom

Sigaud, even when the accusation campaign had failed and he was beating a hasty retreat. When I arrived in Brazil, at the end of May, the first thing I read in the press was a full page that the daily *Folha de São Paulo* devoted to a defense of Dom Sigaud's properties based on "social" considerations: "They accuse Dom Sigaud of being a landowner, defender of capital, and enemy of the poor. But nothing is said about the reason for his buying his estate nor was it revealed that by buying it he made possible the planting of a hundred million trees, giving work today to nearly thirty-five thousand people." And it went on to say that if all the bishops were like Dom Sigaud, social problems in Brazil would be definitively solved. In another story the paper expressed its frustration with the CNBB and the Vatican because they had not intervened against Dom Pedro Casaldáliga. At least they expected intervention from the government, given the obvious dangers of the activities of the bishop of São Félix.

The supporters of the archbishop did not hide their fear that some sanction might arrive from the Holy See or that it would appoint an auxiliary bishop for him in preparation for his retirement. While the controversy still raged, the *Osservatore Romano* published a favorable notice of Casaldáliga's *¡ Yo creo en la justicia y en la esperanza!,* the source of the misquotations with which Dom Sigaud was trying to prove Pedro's crimes; ecclesiastical and political circles interpreted this as an acquittal by the Vatican. And the press headlined it: "Accused bishops absolved"; "Rome criticizes Dom Sigaud." The archbishop fell silent (there was talk of his sinking into a grave depression) and he fled from reporters like a scalded cat; "the matter is closed," he would tell them.

Exactly six months later, when nobody could take the accusations seriously, when in Brazil it was water over the dam ("not even fools believed him now"; "the matter is closed"), the Vatican came on stage with a papal legate and dug up the Sigaud document "to carry out an on-the-spot investigation in order to pronounce a sentence." Since, like Pedro, I understand nothing about diplomacy or diplomatic games in gospel matters, I must confess that I do not find it easy to understand why the Sacred Congregation of the Bishops in Rome, after having in hand for months the accusatory document of Dom Sigaud and the personal information of the president of the Brazilian bishops (who flew to Rome in April to defend the accused bishops before the pope), as well as the personal information of the cardinal of São Paulo, a member of the Sacred Congregation of the Bishops (who also travelled to Rome at the end of May, informed the prefect of the congregation, Cardinal Baggio, and left letters for the pope)—I repeat that I do not understand why months later they suddenly name a personal investigator. And I wonder if this can be a diplomatic tactic to silence the powerful Brazilian choir with their accusations against Bishops Balduino and Casaldáliga; if it can be a diplomatic way of supporting Casaldáliga, denying authority to Dom Sigaud, and closing the case officially with explicit Vatican authority. Or is it rather adding fuel to a fire almost extinguished, to revive it in order to elicit some *monitum* (against the accuser, against the accused?). Or can it be a simple delay in Roman bureaucracy?

The fact is that in Brazilian ecclesiastical circles it has been said that the business of the legate-investigator was thought up by Cardinal Baggio, prefect of the Congregation of Bishops, who is viewed as very close to Opus Dei. The fact is also that this Vatican nomination of a "legate," who turned out to be the archbishop of Terzina, Dom José Freire Falcao, took concrete shape and public voice when the government, pressured by the protests of the Bishops' Conference, was coming to a halt and announced to the country that there was no plan for the imminent expulsion of the bishop of São Félix. So went two rounds in the battle of the forces in power against Bishop Casaldáliga. I agree with Dom Pedro's and Dom Hélder Câmara's interpretation of Dom Sigaud's accusations. Pedro told me: "They reached the conclusion that they could expel me only with the collaboration of the church, and I say that's where Dom Sigaud came into the picture." And Hélder Câmara has written: "When the accusations of Dom Sigaud appeared, the expulsion of Dom Pedro had already been decided upon."

It would be terrible if the powerful in Brazil should consider this to represent the collaboration of the church ("the other power"), when in fact the group involved is the church's most conservative faction. We hope that it will never happen that way, and that Rome will publicly see justice done according to the gospel. Otherwise the church will see its authority discredited where it is now believed in by all persons of good will as a liberating force of the gospel.

To put the frosting on the cake, Bishop Lefebvre appeared in Brazil and showed openly, through the press, his sympathy and support for Archbishop Sigaud, whom he defined as "one of my followers," and he canonized him as "one of the three Catholic bishops in Brazil who is not a communist." The great Lefebvre has again accused the Vatican of "drawing near to communism." If we were to pay heed to this accusation or to try to give it a diplomatic solution, we would have to name a "legate" to investigate the Vatican.

Between the Inquisitor and the Witness

"The archbishop—brother, say I— / for reasons of zeal, no doubt very laudable, / wishes to bring me before a worthy tribunal. / I am, quite evidently, dangerous; woe is me, a communist! . . ."

We are sitting in the courtyard of the training center, and Pedro is reading me verses from his long poem "A half-hopeful, half-melancholy psalm by a bishop accused of communism." The sun falls without mercy on the roofs of Goiás. It is the hour for the obligatory siesta.

"If we give your reply, it would be necessary to publish the Sigaud document also, the text of the accusations," I say to Pedro.

"Do you think it's possible? It's a very long text, confused, with a hundred quotations from my writings, but out of context, and some mistranslated. He makes me say what I don't say. Just by itself it's too long; besides, you'd have to add quite a few annotations. There it is, look at it. Do anything you want with it."

I have thoroughly studied this inquisitorial document, the falseness and slanders of which I have already pointed out. The paragraphs that Sigaud quotes from Pedro's prose and verse have resulted in arousing interest in reading Casaldáliga's original work here in Brazil. But the right to read it has been denied to the citizens and to its author. What publisher will dare to publish it for fear of seeing his company closed by some unappealable order from on high? Nevertheless the most forceful of Casaldáliga's writings have been translated and made public by Dom Sigaud, but out of context and with scandalously false interpretations. To offer the complete text would be to do justice and to open up a path to the truth. But who is interested in this?

I offer here the accusations of Dom Sigaud without the quotations from Pedro's work. This actually strengthens his case because the famous quotations actually weaken his accusations. I also offer Pedro's reply, somewhat shortened. And I arrange both documents so that the reader can perceive a certain dialogue between the inquisitor and the witness. The Sigaud document is inquisitorial with its slashing condemnations and its insistent appeal to the secular arm to punish the criminal. The reply of the bishop of São Félix is that of a witness to truth, because that is his style, the one that Pedro has always preferred and demonstrates in his evangelical willingness to live the faith.

Here are the two statements, summarized but faithful to the original text:

Sigaud Document
Accusations Against Bishop Casaldáliga

I. The sociological position of Dom Pedro
Dom Pedro is a rebel who is against everything and everybody.

II. His political position
The ideas of Dom Pedro Casaldáliga are those of someone who shares in the communist invasion of Brazil. He himself confesses that he is a communist and a subversive.

When the Brazilian government realized the communist orientation of Father Pedro Casaldáliga, it requested information from the Portuguese General Security office about his person. The answer was clear: He follows the political, ideological line of the Third World Christian movement with a socialist orientation. He is on the extreme left (September 5th, 1973).

Influenced by Marxism, he opts for socialism-communism.

He asserts that capitalism is essentially perverse and that socialism can be Christian. He confuses Christianity with communism and subversion.

III. Break with the Brazilian regime

Dom Pedro disagrees completely with the regime that is in power in Brazil. He says: "The Brazilian regime is a Nazi terror plan. The economic powers impose the law and muzzle justice.

Dom Pedro Casaldáliga and Dom Tómas Balduino are the main ones responsible for the tension that exists between church and state in Brazil.

Dom Pedro urges the people to oppose the Brazilian regime, to overthrow it, and to replace it by another, which is the communism that disowns private property. He is a subversive supporter of communism, of guerrilla warfare.

From the time he was in Spain Dom Pedro has been enthusiastic about the communist guerrilla and assassin, Ernesto Guevara, whom communists called Che Guevara. He even dedicated a poem to him. This poem is a communist profession of faith by someone who wants to imitate the murderous guerrilla fighter. . . .

IV. The armed forces

His excellency opposes the civilizing action of the armed forces.

He is antipathetic to them. For him the Brazilian army plays all too well the role of hangman and plunderer. Read what he writes about the military: "Here, in this area, the military are my 'enemies' to the extent that they are the enemies of the people. Because they are at the service of capitalism and dictatorship, because they unquestioningly and obediently carry out tasks of a devious nature, they 'influence projects,' they carry on repression and even torture. I do not quote others, I myself have been a witness to their actions."

V. He is responsible for violence and deaths in Mato Grosso

The climate created in the prelature of São Félix in Mato Grosso by Dom Pedro has brought about the murder of the two missionaries, Father Rodolfo Lukenbein and Father João Bosco Penido Burnier.

VI. He mocks the social programs of the government

And when the government tries to help solve its problems, Dom Pedro misinterprets the governmental initiative.

VII. Opposition to the owners of the large farms

Dom Pedro curses the landowners and breaks relations with them.

VIII. Revolution in the church; the Vatican; nunciatures; structure and tradition of the church

Dom Pedro Casaldáliga condemns the teachings of the supreme pontiff and of the bishops.

He affirms that one must carry on revolution from within the church.

His excellency condemns the Holy See, although he recognizes that the pope is the head of the church. He condemns the sovereignty of the pope, expressed in the State of Vatican City and in the nunciatures.

With other bishops he supports the thesis that the structures of economic, political or spiritual capitalism are idolatry, and amount to a state of sin and death. . . . Therefore, he wants to revolutionize the social doctrine of the church.

He condemns celibacy.

IX. He organized a group of bishops and betrayed the secret of the CNBB.

To make his ideas win out in the National Conference of Bishops in Brazil he organized a group of bishops who follow his orientation and which he calls the No-Group Group.

When the CNBB meets, he organizes parallel meetings that he calls "Lateran Councils," at which many of his friends gather. In 1973 subversive elements took part, among them Alexandre Vanucci.

Dom Pedro Casaldáliga delivered a secret text of a statement of the National Conference of Bishops to reporters from the Folha de São Paulo.

X. Liturgy

He breaks with the liturgy and carries his break to an incredible degree: he refuses to wear the ring or the miter and will not carry the crozier.

On the occasion of the inauguration of the Cathedral of São Félix, Dom Pedro wrote a subversive and violent theatrical work.

At the performance the actors took communion and drank coffee in a sacrilegious communion using consecrated wafers. This sacrilege is the seal of the "new special church of the prelature of São Félix."

The sources that Sigaud quotes as "proofs" of his accusations are the books of Pedro Casaldáliga: *¡ Yo creo en la justicia y en la esperanza!,* and *Tierra nuestra, libertad* (Our Land, Liberty)[2] and also the bulletin of the prelature of São Félix, *Alvorada.*

Dom Sigaud ends his document by condemning Bishop Casaldáliga and canonizing the Brazilian government, the police, and the landowning companies with this statement: "I believe that it is very clear that he embraces and teaches communist doctrines, that he propagates them among the clergy, the religious, and the faithful, creates an atmosphere of class struggle that is making the Araguaia region dangerously tense, to the point where that tension has caused several deaths. There would have been many more deaths if the government, the police, and the great companies had not acted with calmness, prudence, humility, and patience." And he urges: "The Brazilian government must ask the Holy See to remove the bishop of São Félix, Dom Pedro Casaldáliga."

Reply of Dom Pedro Casaldáliga

To the reporter from *O Jornal do Brasil* who went to ask the bishop of São Félix for a public reply to the accusations that Dom Sigaud had made against him, Pedro said: "I would prefer not to answer, now that the matter is with the Holy See. But the publicity that the press has given to the accusations obliges me to reply as a pastoral duty."

Personally, I have nothing against Dom Sigaud, really, states the accused bishop. *I even believe that he is acting with sincere good will and that he is following the dictates of his conscience. For that reason I am not going to engage in polemics with him. I wish to reply to the document presented to public opinion only because it is a biased conglomeration of multilated texts that do not express my thoughts or my attitude.*

This documentation that the archbishop of Diamantina has de-

livered to the press and has presented to the Holy See has for a long time been in the hands of the security forces and I know, from official sources in the National Congress itself, that it was the "hard line" military officers who delivered the documentation to the archbishop.

The bishop of São Félix realizes that he and Dom Sigaud do not think or act alike. He defends pluralism among the members of the church. And after pointing out that "the text quoted in the denunciations is public," already published in Spain and translated into French and Italian, he addresses himself, at the request of the reporter, to the ten chapters of the accusations. These are his written words, which he himself translated into Spanish:

I. Concerning his sociological position

To say that I am against everything and against everybody is an accusation that does not even need a reply. I certainly am in favor of the gospel, for which I am risking my life; above all, I am in favor of the gospel of the beatitudes and the announcement of the good news to the poor, to the prisoners, to the blind. And I am passionately in favor of the Indians, of the farmhands, and of the peons, and also of all the Amazon's natural surroundings that are being destroyed, profaned.

I am also very much in favor of the conversion of the oppressors who, once converted, would stop oppressing.

II. Concerning his political position

I never, never said, in public or in private or in my writings, that I was a communist. Categorically, I am not one (you can underline that). The document's statement, that I have shown myself to be a communist is simply slanderous.

It is also slanderous to say that I confuse Christianity with communism or subversion, or to affirm that I confess to be a follower of Fidel Castro or to say that there are many bishops who chose communism. This is collective slander.

I imagine that the awful fear that a bishop might be a communist arises because communism is considered to be atheistic, materialistic, and essentially dictatorial. Thank God, I believe that there is nothing of an atheist in me, or a materialist, or a sympathizer with any kind of dictatorship.

I said publicly that I am anticapitalist, and I am, and that I choose democratic socialism. This matter would deserve a more detailed answer, because it is complex. Here I'm going to summarize my answer: I understand by socialism the greatest possible participation of all the citizens, and at the greatest possible level of equality, in the wealth of nature and production. To achieve that, obviously, it will be necessary to tear out and destroy the egotism of capital, the privileges of minorities, the exploitation of human being by human being.

Is that utopian? The gospels would be much more utopian. As the Sigaud document itself quotes, I said that, as a Christian, I must go beyond communism, because I believe in transcendence and the parousia.

III. Concerning the Brazilian regime

I never broke with the regime. I was never attached to it. And I never plan to be attached to any regime. I want to be free in order to preach the gospel.

My statement that economic powers impose laws and muzzle justice in Brazil, like other similar statements, is shared by the Brazilian Bar Association, by the official statements of the opposition, and by editorials in numerous papers. These are also the opinions of a great number of intellectuals and of the most distinguished public opinion in the country.

I do not consider myself responsible for the tension between church and state in Brazil. At most I have denounced, with others, the causes that provoke that tension.

I have never defended and I do not now defend armed conflict or the overthrowing of the regime. Nor guerrilla warfare. I am indeed totally opposed to any dictatorship, capitalist or communist, military or civil. I am against all violence and lack of respect for human rights, whether in Latin America or Siberia.

With regard to Che Guevara, whom I admire, as I admire all those who are capable of giving their lives for a cause, I ask that you read the whole of my poem dedicated to him. Similarly, I ask that you also read all of the poems that refer to landowners, to private property, and to other matters quoted in truncated form in the Sigaud document.

IV. Concerning the armed forces

What I say about the military is not an abstract, a priori statement. I have had and now have military friends. What I denounce with regard to the military is the wholly painful experience suffered in the very flesh of the people and the pastoral teams in this prelature.

V. Concerning violence and the death of priests

Accusing me of being responsible for the climate of terror in Mato Grosso, the document tranquilly assumes that I am responsible for the deaths of Fathers Rodolfo and João Bosco. I already told the press, and I repeat it now, that the one truly responsible for all these deaths is Jesus Christ, for whom I also would want to die.

VI. Concerning official programs

I ridicule only those programs that cover up injustices, that protect the large estates, and that try to replace what the people need by what the mighty desire. For that reason, I have denounced many times certain official organizations, the police, and the multinational corporations.

VII. Concerning dialogue and the landowners

I reject dialogue only when it is transformed into complicity. I personally, along with all the pastoral assistants of the prelature, have insisted on sending accounts and documents to a wide variety of authorities in the country and to official organs.

I do not detest the landowners. I do detest, it is true, the huge landed estates. I do not have hatred for any person.

VIII. Concerning the church and the Vatican

I have never, never shown myself to be against the law and the teaching of the supreme pontiff and the bishops, even when I have disagreed, as a pluralistic vision allows me to. I have never disagreed in matters of faith.

To carry on revolution from within the church means precisely to remain faithful to the church, even when recognizing it as sin-

ful and errant. Renewal is a mission of the whole church and a constant call of the spirit of the living Christ. Why would they have celebrated, then, Vatican Council II?

I condemn the bureaucratic-economic structures of the Vatican and I ardently desire greater evangelical freedom for the pope in his mission.

It is not clear to me that the social doctrine of the church favors capitalism, even though this has been, unfortunately, its practice in history, as also, at times, to favor feudalism and colonialism.

Concerning celibacy: I have never, never condemned celibacy. Quite the contrary: I have personally chosen celibacy and up to now I have remained in it with no regrets. I have also counselled many seminarians and religious to accept that choice. But I would be glad to see celibacy and the priesthood separated, so that celibacy would always be a vocation, a free testimony of evangelical oblation.

IX. Concerning the church in Brazil and the CNBB

I have not organized any group of bishops. It's quite a different thing if some bishops meet, with doors open, to discuss together some common problems. The "No-Group Group" does not, of course, exist as an organized group. Its very name indicates that.

I want to make clear that it was not I who delivered the Itaica document to the press and I categorically state that I do not know who did it.

X. Concerning theater and the Eucharist

It is a worse than gross slander to say that the goblet used in the scenic performance of the "inauguration" of the cathedral contained consecrated wafers. The performance was simply theater—a kind of eucharistic play—and its only object was to serve as an introduction to the true Eucharist, which was celebrated later.

PEDRO CASALDÁLIGA
Bishop of São Félix
(O Jornal do Brasil, May 8th, 1977)

What Was behind the Archbishop

"Closed case" or open case, whatever the final sentence, I ask Pedro the most serious question that can be asked about this matter:

"What's behind Dom Sigaud?"

He brushes back his hair nervously and explodes. "Dom Sigaud is only an episode. So am I, the bishop of São Félix; I'm an episode. You've got to open your eyes wide and take in the whole horizon, the entire panorama of the Brazilian church, the Brazilian people, the whole Latin American people and church."

He reflects for an instant, head lowered, and then stares at me: "Look, I have the following impression: that I and the prelature of São Félix have come to be a symbol, a sign of contradiction. (I want to believe before God that it is an evangelical sign. In the gospel it's very clear, all that about being a sign of contradiction.) Because we are in Amazonia legitimately, and it is in Amazonia that the battle of the present conflicts rages most freely. Don't forget that we're in Brazil. That means we're in a world that, besides being capitalistic, is dependent, colonized in the past and now and forever.

"National and multinational interests are centered on Amazonia in a special way. It happens that the Amazon region was the Green Hell, as they said. Concretely, Mato Grosso, all this, the extensive territory of our prelature and its surroundings, was a world unknown to Brazil itself. You know that they even tried to bring thousands or millions of Japanese here to fill these empty lands of Amazonia. But the time came when they discovered the potentialities of these immense regions. The world was horrified at the prospect of finding itself without oxygen, and Amazonia became the world's green lung. Above the land and below it, for if they were looking for oxygen above, they were also looking for mineral riches below. And on the ground level the possibilities of cattle raising beckoned. That is, capitalism, dependent on one part of Brazil and colonizing another part—in which the multinationals were the big gamblers—was especially interested in Amazonia. The capitalists had the governments on their side. They especially had the Brazilian government on their side. And they went on making the plans that we all know, of land exploitation with all its chaos of destruction, invasion, unjust and overpowering occupation that despoils and exterminates the small farmers, tenants, laborers, and Indians.

"And it happened that here, in the very center of our prelature, because the circumstances were very acute and very dramatic (I'll explain later), our church felt bound to utter a cry, in a public way, of denunciation. We put ourselves on the side of the Indians, of the small farmers, of the laborers who were left without land and the landworkers or farmhands. That cry was the pastoral letter that I published on the occasion of my episcopal consecration on October 23, 1971, *Uma Igreja da Amazônia em conflicto com o latifúndio e a marginalização social* (An Amazonian Church in Conflict with the Landed Estates and with Social Marginalization). In that document, we, the group who work here, tried to identify the enemy and give him a concrete name. We found the enemy to be, on the one hand, the huge landed estates and, on the other hand, the social marginalization. That cry of a bishop, a cleric, who is still something of a power, especially in countries where there is no other power apart from the government, attracted a good deal of attention; it was a volley that made an impression."

Pedro stops. He smiles, remembering something, and says parenthetically:

"The other day we were joking about whether the church here would be the fourth or the fifth power, and we reached the conclusion that it is the second power—that there is only the power of the government, with the economy behind it, and the power of the church. Then there are the ones that you know, the intellectuals and the press, who have censorship over them, the university people, who now are once again trying to break the imposed silence, but they don't have much strength for that. The workers here can't do anything at all, nor the farmers, much less the Indians, who are a people destined for death. So there remains the church."

"That explains many things."

"Exactly. This church of São Félix, through the word of the bishop, uttered this cry and it automatically aroused curiosity, then anger, and finally enthusiasm in some people and a certain solidarity."

"The international repercussions were very strong. Your pastoral letter was translated immediately into Italian, German, and much of it into English. Since then international agencies have become interested in you and in São Félix. It wasn't too strident a cry, too sensational?"

"I must say, with complete simplicity and realism, that the document was not a superficial cry. The document was quite well prepared. It did not limit itself to saying three or four things, nor did it go into theories, which was not our mission. It explained the reality of the life of the people and added a forceful appendix, well supported by documents 'naming the oxen' as they say in Brazil: the concrete names of the landholding enterprises and of the gentry who were in them and behind them, bankers, military officers, ministers, natives and foreigners; the crimes of the estates, of their overseers, of their owners, of police bought and sold, of the security forces and all the rest. That got a lot of attention. It was a scandal (in the evangelical sense of the word), and from then on, as a bishop, I found myself as you were saying, a little on a pedestal and a little in a pillory."

Facing us, I notice a flowering bush, wound around and clinging to the arcade of the brightly lit courtyard of the Goiás leadership center. Its huge leaves range from green to blood red.

"It was after the scandal of that cry that the raising of consciousness took hold and spread in the midwest of the country and in several other corners of Amazonia. Meetings were held. The Commission on the Rural Ministry (CPT, *Comissão Pastoral da Terra*) was organized, as also the Indigenous Missionary Council (CIMI, *Conselho Indigenista Missionário*). The latter devoted itself directly to the hopeless plight of the Indian peoples, guided the consciences and the work of missionaries to the Indians, and grappled with the governmental policies regarding the indigenous peoples of Brazil. The CPT completed this mission, concerning itself with the laborer—the migrant worker, the landless farmhand, the "touched" workers, as they are called here, expelled from a huge landed estate *(latifúndio),* the peon bereft of the help that labor laws could provide.

"Besides all this, major and minor conflicts occurred daily, the struggle with this estate, the struggle with that one; for example, the very concrete case of the Codeara Company. Of course, because they were conflicts with persons in high places, and because they were conflicts involving the church, and specifically a bishop, there were national and international repercussions. It was, hence, necessary for the more powerful enemies, the ones with vested interests, to find a scapegoat. I don't know to what extent I was that figure. Perhaps, in addition to what I said or wrote (given the scope that our cry had when it was published), there was the fact that I am a foreigner and therefore more vulnerable. The fact is that they gradually zeroed in on a persecution against us that has shown itself in various ways since then. You know that they first tried to prevent me from being consecrated bishop. And it's curious that it was one of the great landowners who tried it, a superintendent, as he's called here, a kind of general manager of a great landholding enterprise, the Bordón, to be specific, of which one of the mainstays (one of the most important), is the father of the 'Brazilian miracle,' the ex-minister of finance. This superintendent, Mr. Leite, went to the nunciature to block my episcopal consecration; he was accompanied by a priest, a religious whose name I shan't mention, who also played that game."

Evening falls. In the deep blue sky there burst forth the first rockets announcing the village fiesta. It is the conclusion of the popular novena to the *"Divino,"* as they call the Holy Spirit here.

"Following that, within the national church there was created a climate of renovation and commitment, spearheaded by one bishop after another. Unfortunately the bishops were to be almost the only ones who had voice and vote, not only in public opinion, but also within the church, which is always excessively hierarchical. Several of those bishops had already gone through everything, like Dom Hélder, Dom Fragoso, Dom Valdir—military interrogations, threats, and the like. They and other bishops (the famous 'group' that Dom Sigaud denounced as if it were a conspiracy) and some of the more committed local churches gradually sparked a renewal of awareness and commitment that to a certain extent might seem parallel to the general, slower, more bureaucratic progress of the bulk of the church of Brazil, even of the CNBB itself, of the whole of the Episcopal Conference. It aroused suspicions, bickering, opposition, and persecution by the big shots, those who had wealth, those with civil and military power, the National Security, the organs of the SNI—the famous National Information Service that I said before is like the CIA here in Brazil—and also the powerful in the church itself. The hierarchy felt shaken, because, as is natural, you can't touch one thing without touching the other. They were clearly aware that when we entered into commitment with the people we automatically upset—right?—overturned everything in the church, its categories, its organization, its ways and manners."

A flock of green parakeets squawks across the courtyard, whirls about the top of a tree, and flies off happy and strident. And they stirred to anger the parrot in the cage. In Brazil, in the vicinity of every conversation there is a parrot, a macaw, or some parakeets. After laughing at the interruption, Pedro continued.

"Of course, all that must be viewed in a post-Council climate. Let's not be naive—Vatican II is just beginning in many places. And Medellín. Medellín has scarcely begun anywhere. If many haven't yet ingested the theory of Vatican II and Medellín, much less have they adopted the practice. I believe that all those things together provoked the search for a scapegoat. And it didn't fall on me alone, but on several others also. On me fell a series of special circumstances that played their part. For example, the fact of having published those two books, the credo and the poems, which provided Dom Sigaud with what he calls the 'proofs' of my 'communist' identification. Well, Dom Sigaud was 'used.' Because we know, even from information supplied by deputies of the federal chamber, that it was the hard-line military who provided the material for Dom Sigaud. There are even lawyers of the Justice and Peace Commission who say that they can see evidence of two hands in the document: a canonical hand typically ecclesiastical and old-world, and a hand typically policelike and military. We already knew, through long experience, that the SNI, the military, and other organs were collecting everything that we were writing or saying, even in the liturgical celebrations that have been held in the prelature for one reason or another. That is to say that Dom Sigaud was a recorder and a speaker. We know that they (landowners, government, security, military) had several times tried to get me expelled. They reached the following conclusion, which was worked out in the War College itself, the Gregorianum of the armed forces: there was no way to expel me through normal channels. In short, as I've already told you, I was a power, too. I am a bishop; there is the Vatican, there is diplomacy, there is public opinion, national and international.

"They then saw that the only way to expel me (we know this through someone in the War College) was by enlisting the assistance of the church. And that, say I, is where Dom Sigaud comes in. Just as, in some respect, the nunciature itself came in, directly or indirectly. And, as you can see in the accusations, they wanted to work up a portrayal of my position and that of our church, including also Dom Tomás because of his work with the Indians and because he has always supported the prelature of São Félix. He has been one of those committed bishops who have been much concerned with raising the level of consciousness. The grassroot communities were also involved; they represented a sharpening of consciousness by the people and a mode of organization that frightened government officials, who had already put an end to every political party that could mean real opposition, to every kind of political association. If they had put an end to student organization, and if a free press no longer existed, it was only logical that they should be frightened to see the birth of a force at the grassroots even though it sprang from the gospel and lived as a church. Those were the accusations. And all that was, in my way of thinking, what was behind Dom Sigaud."

"Dom Sigaud was used. Putting that to one side, what could be said of the *person* of Dom Sigaud?"

"Well! We might say that there was some reason for his lending himself to this game. Because he was one of the founders of the TFP, an archconservative movement, reactionary and militant, which you also have in Spain under the name of some kind of Covadonga Culturist Society, and which, as you know, is in Chile and other Latin American countries. And because Dom Sigaud is also a man of means, he has repeatedly shown what is at the core of his accusations: his concern over my attacks on private property; and he asks me for a profession of faith on this matter. We may recall that Dom Sigaud wrote a book that was famous at one time, *Agrarian Reform, a Problem of Conscience,* opposing agrarian reform of course, and the students of the time said the book should be called 'Conscience Reform, an Agrarian Problem.' Many other things have been said about him; it does not seem to me charitable to divulge them. I maintain what I have repeatedly said: that I bear not the slightest resentment toward Dom Geraldo Sigaud."

Will an Evil Sowing Bear Good Fruits?

I have read that the CNBB thinks that a primary objective of the Brazilian government in pursuing the scandal of the accusations of Archbishop Sigaud was to silence the latest document of the plenary assembly of the Episcopal Conference, ("Christian Demands of a Political Order,") which was about to be published at that time. It was a document that frightened the government. Dom Tomás Balduino and the cardinal of São Paulo have told me that they think this is true. I ask Pedro if he shares that view.

"Yes, I think the same as they. It is now clear that the government's tactic is to answer one blow with another. To a document from the bishops it responds with a foul blow to the church, with an accusation, with imprisonment, etc. This was seen very clearly in the arrest and torture of Father Maboni and in the expulsion of Father Fontanella. And it is significant that, without any sort of prior arrangement, the CNBB, other bishops in other parts of the country, and I, in this backwoods of the world, do agree to a large extent in our statements to the press to the effect that one of the principal objectives of the accusations of Dom Sigaud was to make a lot of noise and to send up a smoke screen to hide the CNBB document. It is very significant that the government has not said a single word against that document, when it might have had many words to say. It preferred to create a scandal: one bishop accuses other bishops, one part of the church is communist, the bishops don't listen to one another. It is evident that they have tried to distract the attention of the public."

What is going to be the result of that war that captured public attention for half a year? Is anything positive left behind it, will it have negative fruits, or will it pass over like a summer storm? Pedro answers my question:

"Perhaps there'll be nothing more left than what is left on the shores of the Araguaia River after the floods."

His quick, totally negative response leaves him unsettled. He reflects a little and adds:

"On second thought, I dare say that many positive things will be left. And I don't say this hoping against hope but with a quite realistic hopefulness. Each time the cross comes into one's life, or into the life of the church, it sends us—cleaned, purified, shaken up—back to the sources, to the authentic mission; it makes us rethink things, line them up, be wary of being swept to one side or the other, or of being used."

"To be specific: what positive things has it meant to you?"

"Well, look, it has awakened an enormous solidarity, which is a real communion. You have seen this in many of the letters that have been arriving. Many of them showed a wish to be committed to the people and to detach themselves from the powers of this world. It has accentuated a kind of consciousness of the collective martyrdom with which our whole church feels itself persecuted, in the best evangelical sense of the word.

"It also seems to me positive that it has deflated the balloon of unending rumors: it is clear that everything that they wanted maliciously to prove against me, by reading between the lines and excising the convenient little words they were looking for, and then blew up in the voluminous pages of *O Jornal do Brasil,* has come back down to a few truncated texts, to very obviously biased interpretations, or simply to not knowing how to read a poem. Nothing more.

"It also seems to me a positive fruit that the hierarchy felt itself touched in its class honor. This would not be positive in itself, but it's an ill wind that blows no good, and the church has reacted quite well. Of course, Dom Sigaud or his mentors used a bad tactic when they went so far as to say that there were not just two communist bishops but fifty-one and perhaps eighty; notice, almost a third of the angels fallen, a third of Brazilian bishops communist. The thing was so ridiculous that not even fools believed it.

"Also positive is the fact that it has sensitized the sectors that I call 'frontier.' (The 'frontier' is where certain of us church people meet persons who either left the church out of disillusionment or believe they lost their faith, perhaps, or people who haven't reached the church yet or who are beginning to approach a new church, a different, Vatican II, Latin American church of freedom, committed to the poor, to the Indians.) That frontier world has felt itself shaken again, in the best sense of the word, even made enthusiastic."

I have in fact seen the solidarity, the commitment with which wide sectors of the church have reacted. I have read letters, documents, manifestos, and declarations of solidarity with Dom Tomás and Dom Pedro from bishops, priests, religious (entire groups of priests, entire provinces of religious institutes), from intellectuals and students, from communities, meetings, congresses, and even politicians, deputies and senators. I have seen some reactions of those "frontier" people. Like someone who writes to Pedro that he believes in the "dream" of Jesus, in the kingdom, because he sees that there is a church in São Félix that is fighting for him, risking everything.

"I forgot to mention to you another positive fruit that is now a kind of mania of mine, but that I think is quite correct. We're demythologizing—thank the Lord!—the supposed unity of the bishops. We have an obsessive anxiety to *seem* united, much more than to *be* united. In a way similar to the way in which the government of Brazil is very concerned about saving its image abroad and is very little concerned about saving the people of Brazil. There is in the hierarchy a concern about saving an apparent unity that, as Héctor Borrat wrote very accurately in *El Ciervo* (The Stag), has nothing to do with *koinonia,* with true communion. I see that events such as this one—the accusations of Dom Sigaud—demythologize the *appearance* of unity that the bishops insist on presenting as real. If we are not really united on certain things, why appear to be? When they handed out the final sheet for the evaluation of the latest episcopal assembly, I put down as a negative point the obsession with that apparent unity, urging that we be more simple, and that we accept, confess, and defend pluralism, and that we even recognize our defects of disunity so that the people will know them and help us, help us to reform in all ways necessary.

("What a change, Lord, what a conversion! In something that ought to be so normal, because it is so evangelical.)

"Negative? If I am to be sincere with you I must tell you that, in spite of the complications that it is bringing us, I see nothing really negative in this whole matter. For me the only negative thing is the fall of poor Dom Sigaud. I don't believe that the ridicule that has fallen on certain political chiefs is negative. But there *is* a negative effect in the dulling of the impact of the CNBB document, 'Christian Demands of a Political Order.' And we have lost time in chattering when we should have used it on other things. And we have distracted people from more essential and more serious things. And this we all—but especially the people—pay for."

Outside, the people sway and sing along the streets of Goiás, in procession. There is music, and bursting rockets suddenly light up the night. They are the "gyrations of the *Divino*."

We rest.

I read that long poem, "gently melancholic, a little ironical, but full of hope," that Pedro wrote as a first reaction to the accusations of Dom Sigaud. Pedro always had a good sense of humor and irony. He had always been wily. Now humor and irony are for him an imperious and vital necessity. His poetry has become more colloquial, tinged with humor and irony, and somewhat romantic. "In verse," he says, "one whistles what one can't manage to say in crude prose." I can't resist offering a good-sized fragment of this long poem in which Pedro whistles about very serious things:

> The matter is so serious
> that it must be carried to Rome
> > to the Rome of the Caesars, the Rome of the Popes,
> > as the oldest known custom.
> It must be carried to Rome,
> via diplomatic channels, by sacred assumption.
> Or it must be carried on one's back,
> like one of many crosses, with no great heroism.
> As one carries a child, a wounded man, a hoe.
> Or like a banner of natural green,
> apace with many others,
> > natural banner of the Third World, walking palm tree!
> > with the green hope —
> very natural, very high —
> that we shall all be,

a little,
each day
   —Vatican II, Vatican II, Jerusalem I, Bethlehem,
   Bethlehem I —
more free, more human, more brotherly, more renewed:
the faithful, the little ones above all;
even the bishops
   once again fishers of horizons,
   once again tanners of the gospel,
   once again beheaded, unmitered, in the main
      squares of the Empire, to give testimony.

We have celebrated our last Eucharist in this house—of thanksgiving, of commitment to bear witness, of petition to the Spirit. We have been accompanied by some nuns who have together given thanks to the Lord for having bishops like Dom Pedro in Brazil. Also sharing the Eucharist were María (the kind, the gentle María-Marta of this house), another good friend with the name and face of a prophet, and a Canadian religious who has come to interview Bishops Tomás and Pedro about their struggle with Canadian multinational corporations.

This Eucharist has brought to a close the first dialogues with Pedro, inevitably reflecting their context, the hue and the heat of the conflicts that now fill the scene and the life of this bishop subjected to suspicion and persecution by the military government of Brazil and by the most archconservative sector of the church. They are battles in the eternal war.

This has been the preamble of our dialogues in Mato Grosso. Early tomorrow we shall leave this hospitable refuge of Goiás. Dom Tomás will return from his rural communities, where he has been making pastoral visits, and he will take us in his little plane to São Félix. The fifty hours on the bus will be reduced to a three-hour flight. And Maxi, who has been seeing doctors, will take advantage of the opportunity and return with us to his Porto Alegre parish.

When I go to bed, the town is still gyrating. I hear the songs, the music, the burst of the rockets. And nearby I hear Pedro, wakeful in his words, as always, answering the questions of the Canadian visitor.

"The land becomes, is, has always been the first problem."

3

Who Is the Enemy?

Land and Greed

The day has dawned for flying and scrutinizing from above the greedy earth of Mato Grosso. The whole sky is light.

To the rustic airfield has also come the Canadian reporter, who does not want to miss the chance to report on the two "communist" bishops leaving in the little red plane of Dom Tomás (it *had* to be red!). Dom Tomás has been using it ever since he was a missionary among the Indians before becoming a bishop. When he has to leave the plane in small airfields that have no closed hangar, a man watches over it all night to prevent any trouble.

A mechanical failure on take-off forces the bishop-pilot to aim for the highway, but the failure is corrected and we rise again without having to touch the asphalt.

We fly over the wrinkled and gently green mountains of Goiás.

The limitless and very flat horizon hardly allows us to make out the gateway to the "Green Hell," wild and distant Amazonia.

Having passed over the State of Goiás, we see close up the interminable plain of Mato Grosso, carpeted with luminous greens, furrowed by rivers that, beneath the sun, look like broad ribbons of silk. "We are in the geographic heart of Brazil," Pedro shouts to me.

The great fluvial artery of this whole zone is the Araguaia, a river of majestic body with numerous arms, with immense islands. "That Araguaia, free, and so well loved!"

The forest and the glades begin to resurface from the flooding of the rains, which have been endless this year. Great lakes still remain, gigantic ponds, streams, boggy areas drowning the trees. "As if here the hand of God had not yet separated the waters from the lands." Shouting above the roar of the motor, Pedro opens to me the secrets of this lovely mysterious world.

Extensive grasslands. The cattle, diminutive, are the rightful dwellers in these glades violated by the insatiable greediness of the landowners. This farm, that farm. I understand now—it is right before my eyes—the curses and the blessings of Pedro's poems: "Cursed be the big estates / except for the eyes of their cows / . . . / Blessed be the earth / worked and owned by all."

Pedro shouts to me: "In no time at all, this will all be covered with fire, drowned in smoke. When the waters leave, they will burn miles and miles of forest and woods for the big estates." The greed that the big estates flaunt is fatal to this virgin land and to its poor inhabitants. The small farmers who have lived here for ten, twenty, thirty, forty years ("homesteaders" who thus legally took possession of their land) are seized by the tentacles of the all-powerful landowners, and like it or not, always forcibly, they are despoiled. Pedro wrote in verse of the passions and sufferings caused by the violation of these lands: "Land, love, and greed. / Land of tillage. / Land of big estates. / Land of highways. / Land of tombs."

I see a white heron hovering over the green like an immaculate banner. "Peace that comes in its own time." The herons of Pedro's poems! He has sung of all these creatures in the sorrowful and exultant verses of his "Primordial Cry."

We are going to fly over the Araguaia through the stretch where the giant takes into itself the River of the Deaths: "This beautiful, scarcely rippled flowing / of dark green honey." Pedro tells me: "It's called River of the Deaths *[Rio das Mortes]* because of the many Indians they say have been killed in the lands bathed by this river." The waters that this river brings to the Araguaia, clean waters, deep, dark, and green—"the tame green waters"—form a long, narrow band amidst the earthy red waters that the Araguaia bears at this time because of the rains.

We come down a little over the bed of the Araguaia. The broad river begins to bare itself to show the golden flesh of its banks, its dazzling sand.

In the distance, on the left bank, can be seen the humble "episcopal see" of this enormous prelature of Mato Grosso, the town of São Félix. I try to imagine the borders of the 58,000 square miles of the prelature, with the Xingú River on the left, the State of Pará up above, and on the right, from south to north, like a wide trench, the Araguaia. On the other side of the river is the gigantic Banana Tree Island *(Ilha do Bananal)* with its capital Santa Isabel, and the luxurious Kennedy Hotel, now in decline— "miscarried"—a place familiar with important and disquieting arrivals of private aircraft, and meetings and banquets of the great greedy ones of these lands.

I try to picture to myself all the towns scattered over the prelature, lost within Mato, tucked beside the threatening forest or anchored downstream: Luciara, Tapirapé, Santa Terezinha, Ribeirão Bonito, Porto Alegre, Canabrava, Pontinópolis, Serra Nova, San José, Santo Antônio. I shall soon meet their inhabitants, homesteaders, retirees, peons, Indians, suffering people whose struggle I know from afar and whose songs I recall under the roar of the motor of this little plane: "We are a people of humankind, / we are the people of God, / we want land on the earth: / we already have land in heaven. . . ." This is the hymn that Pedro wrote with a knife tip on a wild banana leaf—that we keep in our Salamanca house—on the day that the town of Serra Nova won its new common land (the bishop and a youngster acted as water-boys for the woodsmen). It is now sung in all the rural parts of Brazil as a "Hymn of the Rural Community."

I take a last look from above at these lands before the plane heads for the São Félix landing strip. I remember with emotion the heroic defense of the rights of the poor robbed of their lands that Pedro and his co-workers waged. He gave expression to their situation in these verses:

> This is our land:
> Freedom,
> everyone!
> This is our land,
> land of everyone,
> brothers and sisters!
> The land of the people
> who walk through her
> barefoot and poor.
> We are born on her, from her,
> to grow with her,
> like trunks of spirit and flesh.
> Who are buried in her
> like seeds
> of ashes and spirit,
> to make her fruitful like a mother-wife.
> Who surrender to her,
> each day,
> and surrender her to God and the universe,
> in thought and in sweat,
> in their joy
> and in their grief,
> with their gaze
> and with their hoe
> and with their verse. . . .

Pedro has told me: "The land becomes, is, has always been the first problem." Now this problem brings cruel suffering; the few little people who have land are losing it and the big owners pile it up, conniving to despoil it.

The Enemy Is Not the CIA

Two swift swoops over São Félix plunged me, right and left, into its rustic houses and its streets. Then all the impressions came to me all at once. The red earth of the landing strip. The sun and the air, blazing, wrapping me in fire. The hugs, the greetings, Pedrito, Irene, Cecilia, Vera. In the town, the variety of houses, made of palm leaves, of adobe, of bricks bare or whitewashed. The new mission house, spacious and clean, the work of Pedro, like the new cathedral built with materials from the countryside. The courtyard of the hammocks. Geralda, the macaw with a very long tail, green, yellow and red. The great pile of letters and magazines on Pedro's small desk. The relaxing music. The Indian presence on the walls (Carajá jars, crowns of Xavante feathers, photographs of Tapirapé). Matos, Lulú from Serra Nova, the teachers Zé Wilson and Isabel, Giselda, the other friends, the picturesque police chief of Porto Alegre, the people who come and go, day and night, at any hour (the house is the town here and the town is the house). The reporters from German television Channel 2. (Two months ago the ones from Channel 1 were here.) The farewell to Dom Tomás, who flew off in his red bird taking some fresh fish from the Araguaia to his people. ("Dom Tomás and Dom Pedro are twin souls," Sister Irene said to me as the plane rose.) The excursions with Pedro. The old man dying in the hospital, the newly arrived young doctor, the good people at the doors of houses, greeting, embracing their bishop, talking. The climb to the woods on the knoll behind the house, in mud up to our ankles, just so the Germans could film the town from above. The prayer before the old familiar shrine, now set among tropical plants and trees. The bicycle ride through São Félix with Sister Irene, the old gymnasium, the wide streets of dusty earth, prostitutes' row, and the Araguaia, ever-present, like the main street and the fish market. The nights with no light save for a queen-size moon. The rice and black beans, the bananas and the tasty Araguaia fish. And the roosters that crow all night, in stereo.

On the third day—on the third night, to be precise—Pedro takes me to the church. "Here they will let us talk in peace."

The very first day there, I went to visit the newly-built "cathedral." Bright, simple, spacious, almost bare; a first glance takes in everything. It is the house of the people, a house of prayer and of meetings. Rectangular, with two false partitions creating three spaces: the entrance, the nave, and—behind the altar—the sanctuary chapel. The twelve columns of the nave, as well as the altar, sanctuary chairs and credence tables, are carved from cinchona tree trunks, natural and bare, with irregular, twisted, vinegar-colored veining. The benches are low, very simple. Palm-leaf candleholders, woven by Tapirapé Indians, hang over the altar. At the focal point is the Crucified, with an Indian Mary—maternal Guadalupan—to one side, in a huge painting mounted on a tree-trunk column and footed with plants. Farther back, the quiet prayer-space before the sanctuary has low tree-trunk stools, more plants, and a Carajá baptismal laver: "Baked white mud / of virgin clay— / womb of baptismal water— / that pagan hands kneaded / to beget Christ."

Now, entering the church with Pedro, at night, there is no light except that from the little oil lamp of the sanctuary and the lantern that we bring with us. Leaving the sanctuary behind, in the first corner of the nave we sit down at a tiny table, Pedro and I, leaning over the tape recorder by the flickering light of the oil lamp.

"Two questions have concerned me since I saw these lands that the big landowners are snatching from the small farmers. First: Is there any solution? Second: Who is the enemy?"

"Solution? Look, there would be one if we had the kind of politics that would give heed to the little man, that would control and limit a little the interests of the big companies, and that would clean up all that needs cleaning up in the different administrative sectors, beginning at the top and ending with the last of the mayors. That would be quite a thing! Honestly, even in economic terms (notice that I'm even talking from a capitalistic frame of reference) it's the small farmers who are the real producers. This has been demonstrated by experts; I'm not inventing it. Two or three years ago, if I'm not mistaken, the magazine *Visão* (Vision), and I think also *Opinião* (Opinion), published a very interesting account of this. It's the small farmers who supply the agricultural products that the people consume. If you suppress all the truck gardens and small farms on the outskirts of the big cities, you'll see what they'll be eating in Rio, in São Paulo, in Goiânia, and other places. And look at what's happening here on the plantations—the poor eat rice. Where does it come from? And the black beans? And the flour? From the homesteaders the big landowners are trying to rob of their lands! This is clearly a very poor region, but if it had a different political orientation, if the small farmers were helped. . . .

"Look, Father Francisco Jentel was saying some five or six years ago that if they gave to the small producer one percent of the subsidies that are squandered on those gigantic corporations that frequently aren't even Brazilian. . . . We are giving the money to people who don't need it, to people who already have it and who, moreover, waste it, and some of them don't even invest here the subsidies they are granted. If they gave just one percent to the small farmers, all the problems of all the homesteaders of Amazonia would be solved—the indispensable substructures for technical and agricultural assistance, health, schooling, even roads. With just one percent of what they have given to the great enterprises! Here Volkswagen is getting millions, just like Bardón, Codeara, Suemesul, etc., etc."

I follow through: "You took advantage of Dom Sigaud's accusations to retaliate with a blow of your own. Apart from the many clarifications that you made, you also brought out a major accusation: you accused the CIA of trying to strangle the very vigorous church in Latin America, deeply committed to the poor, by means of a perifidious strategy program worked out for several countries. Is the CIA the enemy?," I ask Pedro.

He replies: "In the first place, I did not report anything really new, although it *was* little known and very little reported in any official way by the bishops or, of course, by the episcopacy as a whole. The program of the CIA, full knowledge of which was made known to us Brazilian bishops in our last plenary assembly, is really a program of harassment and strangulation against the most open and most committed church in Latin America. They planned this for several countries—let's say for the whole continent. It was in Bolivia that an explicit method was discovered. It was published in some European journal or bulletin, in Paris if I'm not mistaken, and some newspaper also published it. Nevertheless, I would like to clear things up a little: the CIA is not *the* enemy. The CIA, and all the CIAs, are the instruments, the means, used by the enemy. The enemy is capitalism. Let's say this quite clearly, and without fear that the fence sitters, who are neither rightists nor leftists (and who probably aren't anything at all), will accuse me. Let them accuse me. I feel I have enough truth on my side to say what I say. The enemy is capitalism."

"Explain yourself," I ask him.

"You know that capitalism is by nature colonialist, don't you? Capitalism by nature creates dependence, between one person and another, between one people and another, between one continent and another. This is evident, isn't it? Then what could the CIA be, what could all the CIAs be, except an instrument? The same applies to the various organs of information and repression, the famous organs of National Security, which constitute in Latin America, as you know, a veritable political idolatry and an absolute power without any possible appeal or recourse. They are instruments of capitalist imperialism. The capitalist countries, with the United States at the top, of course, lost their colonies in Asia and Africa one after another, the territories that they could most easily exploit but where they were then challenged by attitudes of freedom, of self-identity, of independence. They have had to turn more and more toward Latin America. Latin America had been independent for many years, but for many years it continued to be colonized.

"And the United States (this is known, this is in the talk, in the song, in the theater, in the humor, in the anger, and in the blood of all the peoples of Latin America—you've noticed it)—the United States is the great enemy in all this. It is obvious. The United States and those other clearly capitalist countries. Politically they might seem to have a certain appearance of democratic socialism and all that, but it is very relative and very deceptive because often the economy goes in one direction—the one that gets results!— and politics goes in another direction with labels that are fine but false. That's why in politics you must always be very radical to really get to the causes. I don't at all believe in reformation. I have very little belief in neodemocracies."

He is speaking in a low voice, almost a whisper, but with great conviction.

"At any rate, the United States and those capitalist countries that were obliged to retreat from Asia and Africa needed to make sure that the Latin American market could not escape them, the raw material of Latin America, the subsoil of Latin America, the millions of workers, cheap, easy hand labor of Latin America, as well as the market for imports. Above all, the land, the infinite expanse of land in Latin America—this Amazonia that I have called a reservation of the multinationals—and it is, it really is. Notice, while many things are devalued by overproduction, the land continues to be prime wealth, with extraordinary potential. And capitalism knows this very well. It was logical that they should make extreme efforts to get possession of Latin America. And the Latin American people had no way to resist because of their centuries-old neocolonial dependence, and because most Latin American peoples were in the hands of dictators or oligarchies, for example, the typical family oligarchies that have already been denounced in famous novels and films.

"But a different force sprang up, 'free' (at least, in quotes, right?), with an extraordinary potential for freedom—the church. A force that, moreover, was hard to argue with because the Latin American people are religious, Christian, Catholic. It would have been much easier to challenge communism, materialistic, atheistic, and all that. It was much harder to challenge the church. That's why it was necessary to reorganize repression, in a very sophisticated way, expressly against the church, against its most popular and most vital activities. For example, that CIA program, touching on a sensitive point of nationalism distinguishes knowingly between native bishops and priests and foreign-born bishops and priests. And they know how to appear very friendly toward certain priests and bishops and to denounce and persecute only another type of priest and bishop. They know very well how to label as communist anyone they choose. And they can also, picturesquely, if it were not so tragic, pick up the old legacy of the mother countries off there in Europe, can't they? Everything was being done and is being done (*is* being done, notice, the great speeches of marshals and generals of today use that kind of language), in the name of Christian civilization. Not very amusing, is it, that Christian civilization is being used to fight against the gospel? I have already said many times—I have even said it in public—and I have written that one is almost ashamed to be a Christian and to be Western and Spanish because of that colonialism and neocolonialism that exploit the words that are used by a brutal, criminally sophisticated repression."

We heard a clicklike sound behind us. We looked at each other. We stopped and listened. Nothing. "Some bug that hit the sanctuary lamp," Pedro said. And he went on.

"The analysis that I am giving you (and this analysis is not just mine, it's obvious, it's common knowledge, to any who open their eyes and see what is really happening) and the very force of capitalism that creates dependencies show that things cannot happen in any other way. Well now, what journals that are a little open and awake are saying, the lists of the dead, the ghostlike lists of 'the missing,' the endless lists of the imprisoned, of the tortured, of the deported and exiled, the lists of organizations and political groups, pastoral groups, intellectuals, students, who have paid dearly—all give testimony to the persecution perpetrated by capitalism, oppressing and repressing all of Latin America, keeping it from the second, the new, the true independence. I like to recall the beautiful recording of the South American cantata where Mercedes Sosa sings: 'Another emancipation, another emancipation we have to win.' The true independence."

The night is as bright as day. The river, the woods, the town are transfigured under the most brilliant moonlight I have ever seen in my life. They tell me I'm lucky, because I've arrived here with this full moon. For this people that lives in the dark this moon really is "the night sun." These nights truly are "moonlit nights," *noites de luar*: the light of this moon is a celebration.

Tomorrow we shall leave São Félix. We shall go off by boat on the Araguaia to Luciara. Now, while I lie sleepless on this bed that Pedrito has lent me because it has mosquito netting, in the little room I share with the bishop, who is *not* sleepless, I turn over in my mind all my meetings and impressions of São Félix.

The old man whom we visited in the hospital has died. He recognized the bishop when he gave him absolution, but his tired breathing could no longer cope with his rigid body. His wife and his children looked at him sadly without shedding a tear. "Here death is too well known for tears."

The sun was pitilessly scorching the streets, and the dust that was raised was like a fiery smoke.

The police chief of Porto Alegre looked like a cattle rustler in an old western. Tall, spare, pockmarked, with a mustache and a thin scratchy beard. He talked in shouts and laughed with the unbridled force of an animal at Pedro's jokes, with roars and enormous guffaws, throwing back his head and hat and exposing his teeth. The only thing he didn't do was shoot into the air. Maxi has gone with him as far as Porto Alegre, in his old car, because the bus doesn't run today.

Pedro has made a deal with Matos, the boatman, to take us for a few days along the Araguaia as far as Luciara, Tapirapé, and Santa Terezinha. This Matos has a clean look, confident, and the frank handshake (a hug for the bishop) of a faithful friend.

The television crew from Germany has been discreet these days, except during the Eucharist this afternoon. They had been showing up around the house looking for typical moments in the life of the bishop, without making any noise, without interrupting anybody. They were filming the bishop reading letters, sitting at his tiny desk (four spans by two) between the door, the closet, and his bed, in "our" room, where there's not space for another chair; I would sit on the other bed and we would talk. They filmed him talking with a boy and his grandfather, a backwoodsman; they filmed him joking and talking with the people he met in the street and during his visit to the laborers in the brick works.

But at this afternoon's liturgy they filmed frenetically. The townspeople had gathered to give thanks for the twenty-five years of their Bishop Pedro's priesthood. The liveliness of the celebration induced the Germans to turn on their huge camera lamps. The greetings, the readings, with comments by Pedro, the faces of the people singing, the dialogues with the people during the homily, moving from bench to bench, the procession with the offerings, the consecration, the pax, the communion. The camera crew bitterly lamented running out of film when, at the end, all the people went up to embrace the bishop. "We had no idea," the Germans moaned and, much moved, they also embraced Pedro. At the altar Clelio, who is on his way to Luciara, and I accompanied the bishop. Pedro introduced me to the congregation and I felt their affectionate warmth.

Then, under the full moon, we ate the cake that Cecilia baked this afternoon and we drank sparkling wine and refreshments, between songs, making a celebration for Pedro in the courtyard of the hammocks. Pedro sings like a madman, all kinds of songs. I am surprised by his boundless love for singing, which surely must have grown here, in the struggle, like his humor, his irony, like his hope, and his faith. Sharing in the party with us was the head of the German television team. He seems to be one of those men that Pedro meets "on the frontier." The Germans have a great sensitivity for the Third World. Misereor and Adveniat are two German organizations that give aid and finance projects for Third World countries. But I was astonished to see what enormous and choice morsels of Brazil German capitalism is eating up. Will they perhaps give back, in aid, a few crumbs left of what they are carrying off? True aid would be to leave to the Brazilian people what belongs to them and channel it toward the people. It is well known that, for some time, Opus Dei has had some degree of influence on Adveniat and that they are denying economic aid to projects suspected of somewhat leftist or simply liberal ideology. It was repeated to me here, at the CNBB and elsewhere, what I have also been told in other countries, that Bishop López Trujillo, secretary of CELAM (*Conferencia Episcopal Latinoamericana*), a zealous champion of moderation in the Latin American church, seems to have very good relations with Adveniat. Let's not be deceived. As Pedro says, after all, capitalism is capitalism, whether it disguises itself as social democracy or as neo-Catholicism.

The roosters call to one another in the tranquil night. I imagine the moon slivering the Araguaia. The German TV crew will come tomorrow to film the bishop setting out from the pier in the boat.

Through the window I hear the lively voices of the first gymnasium class in the school. It is half past five in the morning.

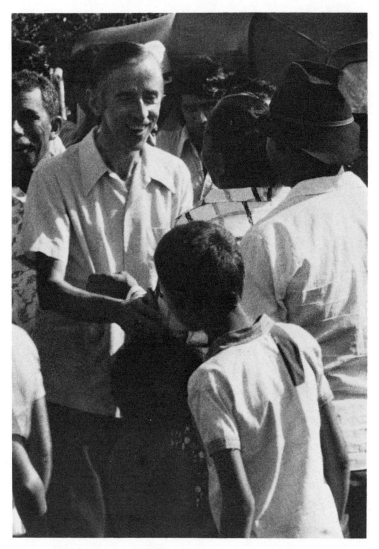

"I certainly am in favor of the gospel, for which I am risking my life; above all, I am in favor of the gospel of the beatitudes and the announcement of the good news to the poor, to the prisoners, to the blind. And I am passionately in favor of the Indians, of the farmhands, and of the peons."

"My life is the Araguaia!
The indescribable river, undecipherable . . ."

4

The Araguaia and Death

The River Is Like a Painting

We cut through the waters of the legendary Araguaia with Matos at the rudder. Up ahead is Clelio with all his bundles for Luciara; in the middle, Pedro and I. On Bananal Island, on the other side of the river, we have left a young man from Rio de Janeiro, a houseguest for a few days, who was out to discover the Mato Grosso. On the pier in São Félix stayed the Germans and their cameras.

Seated at water level, we perceive the immense width of the Araguaia differently. Its banks are like distant green skyscrapers, the dense forest. The waters open out swiftly into branches, canals, arms. And, in the distance, the river extends into that "third dimension" in which forest and clouds blend their watery forms.

There are stretches where the surface ("water-skin-vegetation") gently undulates, and then the waters suddenly strike the shell of the boat like stones. But these waters are almost always quiet, soft, "and the river is like a painting." With his ten years in São Félix, Pedro has much of his life invested in this river, hundreds of hours up the Araguaia, down the Araguaia, in the sun and in the rain, in the rise and fall of the waters. Sensitive, contemplative, poetic, Pedro has in his verses all the variations that life, liberty, and death take on in this his Araguaia, "so dearly loved!"

Matos, astern, reads the water and plots the way. He has to look for the deep channels because the water level drops and the Araguaia leaves long sand banks at the water level.

"A turtle!" and Pedro points out to me the little shell that blends into the gray waters. Matos, who sees everything there is in the river, has already turned the boat. The turtle is dead, moving only with the motion of the waters that are its grave ("and the river is like a painting").

Along the thirty-five miles of the Araguaia that we cover today, Pedro reveals to me the life that hovers around it or hides in the river: the parrots, their names and colors; the other birds, their forms, their flight patterns; the turtles and their nests of countless eggs in the sand; the fishes of all sizes—that "daily bread that is this fertile Araguaia!" I look greedily and I listen. And I let myself be wrapped in the memory of the verses in which Pedro has sensed this mysterious "king of the waters." He has even sung to "the dead tree trunks in the river, floating or fixed, in capricious shapes—arches, muscles, nets, cobras." And he has exalted the living creatures, the various fishes—*murure, pacú, tucunaré*—the seagull, the hoatzin, the *sabiá,* the *manguarí* "the heron at the water's edge at every hour." "And the children bathing / joining the waters, like fishes."

We pass an occasional canoe and we see on the banks the palm-thatched houses of the Carajá Indians, permanent tourists on these beaches.

I am infected by Pedro's passion for the Araguaia. "The rivers are this river: / my life is the Araguaia! / The indescribable river, undecipherable / that looks at itself, accepts itself, possesses itself; / possesses us, / loves itself, thanks itself, and fears itself. . . ."

This river submerges me in the unfathomable, its earthy bed makes me touch life and feel death.

The boat turns into an unlikely canal and we approach the bank until we feel, like a pain, the prow of the boat hitting the sand. We are at the deserted pier of Luciara.

Luciara: Death and Gentleness

"It now has two thousand inhabitants and a few Carajá Indians." Laden with bundles, we walk along a wet open space, almost like a stagnant pond, where the grass grows wild. We are heading toward the poorest quarter. "Luciara, you know, was once a provincial capital; it has a long tradition of bossism and corruption."

The houses are lined up on streets parallel to the river and perpendicular to the river. A perfect grid. These streets are crossed by an occasional cow, and there are broods of hens and a few children, dark, naked, undernourished. "It is now a town pushed into a corner by the big estates." Pedro walks next to me and talks to me in a low voice. "Here the people are being left without land and without work. It's a way-out place that will end up having no way out."

Luciara will stay in my memory like a strange figure between death and gentleness. I see death as I walk with Pedro through all the streets of the town. For quite a while we have the company of Clelio, the young Frenchman who is the parish priest in Luciara.

The bishop and Clelio always greet everyone, then ask questions and listen. Everyone wants us to come in. The houses are of clay and palm leaves, braced by tree trunks lying on the bare ground. Some of the houses are adobe with thatched roofs; only a few are wooden and whitewashed. The people are very simple and affectionate. They embrace their bishop and tell him their sufferings, their problems. At the end of the walk it seems to me that we have made the rounds of death, and I don't know whether to surrender or revolt. I'm overpowered by sadness, anger, and a desperate feeling of impotence.

I have seen death in the sick flesh of these people. Old Nazare has her nose eaten away, her nasal cavities open and fleshless, and her lips very swollen. "Leishmaniasis," Pedro tells me. A microbe destroys the cartilage, opens the flesh and inflames the nose and mouth horribly. It is transmitted by a mosquito. It is contagious. The people, suspecting it may be leprosy, impose a kind of quarantine. With Nazare live her daughter and a newborn granddaughter.

A man, about forty but looking very old, has two fingers of each hand eaten away; he has one foot missing and the stump wrapped in a dirty rag. ("They say it was a snake. You never know.") We sat quite a while in the spacious front yard of his house, in the shade of some gigantic mango trees that his old mother planted when they arrived, almost fifty years ago. They are the only two left in the family. The old woman, with a face all wrinkles but her eyes flashing with life, tells us that she has had a "very ugly" dispute with the authorities because they want to raise her taxes and she won't be able to pay them.

A young black woman has lost her husband only a week ago. The enormous eyes of her three small children look at us with glistening sadness.

A man, standing up, has an attack of malaria. He is one of the many who suffer from it, for malaria is a common illness here in spite of the fact that the fumigators cover the region every year. We met them right here, when they were finishing up at one of the houses.

Seated in the doorway, a pregnant woman with her many children in the front yard, has a terrible toothache and is expecting the doctor to come in a few days. I have not seen one sound set of teeth around here; from the age of twelve Luciarans start losing their teeth without hope and without replacement.

We sit down on an old wooden bench in the middle of the street to chat with a man who is almost lying in the street. I see his swollen ankles and feet, almost open wounds, covered with insects, worms, tiny mosquitoes, swarms of them. Even though he moves his feet or shakes his hand at the insects, they are no longer frightened. He puts up with them. He gets up and brings us the ointment that the doctor ordered for him the last time he passed through the town.

The only person whom I've seen joking and laughing with the

bishop, recalling his past as a rascal, a bully, a gunman ("he was a famous gunman in the region"), is an old man who can no longer walk unaided and who has returned several times from death. He has very thin arms and legs, his whole body burned almost black, with very lively eyes and white hair cut very short. While the old man laughs, I see at his side the pale, freckled face of a woman, with the unmistakable grimace of absence, of madness. And behind me I hear a cackle and a shout: a very small child, with the merriment of a tease, is throwing stones at Tersina, the half-wit.

The children who are playing in the street have bellies swollen with hunger and hookworms. "All the children here have worms." "Pot-bellied with worms. / Yellow with hunger and malaria."

"There's malnutrition, epidemics, malaria, some cases of leprosy, epilepsy. Infant mortality is very high. There is no hospital, no permanent medical assistance. There's just one doctor who stops by for a few hours every two weeks."

Way on the other end of the town, on the last riverside street that has almost no houses and looks out over the countryside, an old lady of eighty-five is preparing the cord to weave a sleeping net, a hammock. The old lady is very sad because her husband has been on the road for four months and she has had no news of him.

We also stopped by to greet Luciara's prostitute, who has her house on the same street. She wasn't at home. Her daughter, sitting on some clothes on the ground, looks at us with her big eyes without even the slightest smile at our greetings.

I have also seen death in the faces of these Luciara children who do not smile. Close to their parents or leaning against the doorjamb, attentive, silent, the children listen without blinking to the grief, the problems, and the illnesses that their parents tell us about, the sadness, the anger, and the helplessness when they tell us that they have no work, no money, that they had to give up their claim for the several years of wages owed to them by the landholding company, which refuses to pay them because, after passing through the offices of who knows how many representatives of law and justice, they are told that there is no written contract. I notice that the children "participate" in their family misfortunes from a very early age, almost as soon as they participate in life.

This is confirmed by Teresa and Aninha, two young women of the prelature of Luciara: "The children take part in grief and death as soon as they are born."

Here, in Luciara, Matos tells us, somberly, of his sadness and his fears. His wife has taken their baby to Campo Grande for another examination. The first test was positive. Leprosy.

After supper, Pedro and I went out into the street. We took a walk. It's hardly seven o'clock and already it's dark. Night falls quickly, as soon as the sun sets. You could say that the light flees from the landscape. I tell Pedro my impressions of that "round of death." He says: "At times I have asked myself very seriously if I exaggerate my attitudes, if we go too far in our struggle in favor of these people, if I am letting myself be carried away by bitterness and anger to the point where I lose objectivity. I have thought a lot about it because the reactions—the accusations of some and the criticisms of others—have forced me to ask myself these questions. But when I get involved once again, here and in other towns, with the real dramas of these people, I see that I'm right, that I don't exaggerate, that we are not going too far. It seems to me that we're not going far enough."

The moon comes out gleaming with light. The whole street is silver and shade. Through the windows and the half-open doors the yellow lights of the oil wicks blink. "People aren't accustomed to going out into the street now. Night falls early, as you see, and since they don't have electricity or television or newspapers, they talk to one another a little and they soon go to sleep. Anyone who may see us walking around at this hour will think we're crazy." And I comment: "When a town has no light, babies constantly come to light." And we go in to sit around the candle, which in our mission house does last a long time.

A young man is giving an account of his serious illness from "worms." "I was sure I was going to die." And he describes his reactions very graphically, the drastic treatment, the slow recovery.

In this house the door is always open, just as it is in São Félix (but in Luciara everything is poorer and more cruel). One arrives, another comes in, several come, sit down, and they all talk. All day and a good part of the night. They come here to relax and to pass the time. This morning a whole family of Carajá Indians came, the women dressed in bright colors, their cheeks and fore-heads painted with circles of black and their coffee-colored legs with beautiful twisting lines. They are bilingual. They have said little, but they are self-confident here. This is also their home.

Now surrounded by the night we huddle around the light that burns on the ground. Our shadows dance when the flame moves, the mosquitoes are a nuisance, and the words are trusting, slow, warm.

The talk is of the backlands, the *sertão,* and of the home-steaders and the harsh struggle they now have to undergo in Lu-ciara. Twenty-nine families of homesteaders have occupied and farmed these lands for thirty years. According to the prevailing Brazilian law, the land is theirs, but the Boavista Bank—power, capital—has become a landowner and is attacking them. It wants their land, one way or another. What it is doing is illegal, but permitted and supported. First they offer them money, they "in-demnify" them at a cheap price and make them sign a paper. If the homesteaders won't sell, warnings rain down upon them, advice, pressures. The bank—the enemy—has invented a curiously in-sulting title, "squatting homesteaders," to imply that the homes-teaders are "squatting" on lands that were probably not theirs and that they must now abandon, whether they like it or not. As "homesteaders" (proprietors, according to the law) they have no written title to their property; the law is mocked, and the home-steaders are defenseless before the monster. If they hold steady, invoking the law, then come the clawings, the violence and mis-fortune, invasion, ill treatment, fire destroying the crops or the houses—all without fear of punishment.

"He has to resist. The homesteader has to resist. He must not sell. He cannot yield: the land is his, and what they want is for him to be a coward."

Few resist. Most of them give in. Here in Luciara the majority has already sold its land at a loss. In no time at all they won't have a cent, or any work, or any more land than just enough to bury them. Up to now only eight homesteaders have resisted, facing up to the big landowner in this unequal and unjust struggle.

"You see?" says Pedro. "That's the land here. The land, the fundamental blessing, is for these people the source of their goods *and* their evils. The blessed earth ought to be their life and it comes to be their death, the cursed land of the great estates.

"They say they saw dead bodies in the lake. They probably were from the company. Peons, you can bet. They were probably demanding their rights."

The conversation shifts inevitably from struggle to death.

"Has there been any news here about four policemen they say were killed in Ribeirão Bonito?

"Nothing. About Ribeirão Bonito, nothing. There's talk about Campo Grande. They say they took to the hospital a young man wounded by a policeman, and that the same policeman went into the hospital and shot him to death."

"They say." "It's been heard." "There's talk." Here the only circulating newspaper is the spoken word. Things are passed from mouth to mouth, with a few details and rumors added. After sifting through various versions, the news is left behind. Several weeks after the first rumor, you find out with some certainty how many have died and where and how.

If death here is untiring, powerful and certain, gentleness is smaller and more discreet. Gentleness is Teresa (a teacher) and Aninha (a social worker), volunteers in Pedro's team in Luciara. Gentleness is in the presence, the look, the welcome, and the voice. They are there, available, they welcome everyone, they smile, they listen, they encourage, they advise, they help, with no watch, no timetable, no provisos, no covetousness, with patience, without clashing, without forcing anything. Gentleness in their faces and in their ways, gentleness also in their unrelenting constancy. True angels of Luciara, at home, in the street, in class, in the backlands that they frequent, awakening the consciousness of the homesteaders. Aninha lost one arm as a little girl, but the other one is enough, and more than enough, for herself and for the others, and for riding horseback into the back country.

Aninha and Teresa are young Brazilian girls. They are not religious nor do they belong to any association. They are lay persons, human beings who believe in the Bible, members of the team of the prelature of São Félix.

Clelio, the young French priest, with his amiable talk and his attentive presence, is also a kind of gentleness, "To be with people is the most that can be done here now." An angel also in Luciara, and at home, with his woodworking skills and other manual arts. Very involved with labor movements, he was himself a laborer before coming to be a priest in Mato Grosso.

I am touched by this gentleness in the midst of this death.

At the end of two hours, the darkness and the music of the Brazilian voices bring sleep to my weariness of today. I think that sleep is also gentleness and death when it removes you, like a drug, from those who go on talking at your side. I surrender to sleep near them, on the other side of the partition, in the bed that Clelio lent me, since everything else here is hammocks, and they say that to learn to sleep in them you need a certain apprenticeship that I don't yet have.

The Latest Accusations

"The homesteader must be firm," one of them was insisting, sitting with us last night. And he added: "But we don't know the law and they deceive us. Eight different men have presented themselves to me already, each one saying that he is the owner of my land. The only people that defend us and teach us are the priests."

The priests and the lay persons in Pedro's team, here in Luciara as in the other districts of the prelature, have had to pay attention to these land conflicts. They have repeatedly given information to and have asked for solutions from all the official authorities and structures. They accompany and encourage the homesteaders, they defend them against the abuses of the landowners and they have had to go so far as to make accusations. And so they have entered into this struggle and into this death.

The most recent accusation was Pedro's statement before the parliamentary commission that is investigating land problems, the CPI, in Brasilia, before the national press. Called to testify, with others, as the bishop of a region with landownership disputes, he collected data and denounced the harassment, pressures, deceit, and other violations of the rights of the people. The greatest uproar resulted from the accusation he made against the three generals of the Brazilian army, Humberto de Souza Mello, Reynaldo Mello de Almeida, and Rosalvo Eduardo Jansen. He accused them of corrupting the mayor of Luciara to turn over to the Codeara Company lands that belong to people who lived in Luciara. It was this famous accusation that apparently put Pedro in danger of expulsion.

The Codeara landowning company (the one that had the skirmish in Santa Terezinha that brought on Father Francisco Jentel's imprisonment and expulsion) goes far in harassment. They are like greedy earth gods, omnipresent, all-powerful, cruel. Codeara's misdeeds filled a whole chapter of Pedro's accusations before the CPI.

The whole session was stormy. Expectations had been roused concerning the figure of Pedro by the accusations of Archbishop Sigaud and by Pedro's audacity: he voiced his convictions and did not spare himself any conflict. After two hours of reading the declaration, followed by a luncheon break, there was a debate that lasted all afternoon, with angry challenges to the bishop. Pedro responded with dialectics and incisive evangelical clarity as only he can do.

The press received copies of the statement of the bishop of São Félix. "Take one," Pedro says to me, "and publish whatever you wish."

The statement, signed June 14, 1977, bears the title: "The Agrarian Question, a Political Question." It consists of three and a half pages of introduction, a body of twenty-one pages of documented accusations regarding specific cases of conflict, and seven final pages of "questionings," disquieting conclusions.

Letting a selection of his paragraphs speak for themselves, I give the floor to Pedro:

"Honored members of this Parliamentary Investigative Commission.

"1) Once again, a statement on the part of the church to a parliamentary commission on land—on the part of the church of Amazonia, specifically.

"In this, as in other human problems and aspirations, the church is fulfilling, well or ill, almost always a little late, its life-saving mission. Through the force of the incarnation, nothing human is alien to Christ, and nothing human must be alien to the people of his church.

"A prophetic mission of accusation and vindication; of a call for change, in certain aspects because the class structures, rural organizations, do not have the freedom and representation that would be necessary to act effectively, and because the public power is not sufficiently interested in a real solution to the problem.

"Naturally, in these statements we make accusations—in the case of 'conflicts' we cannot praise. We present here the griefs of our people that the people themselves ought to be able to present. We speak not as technicians but as witnesses.

"I myself do not speak either as a native or as a foreigner but as one who was officially summoned to speak to this CPI.

"2) I present a series of specific cases to add to many other cases presented to this CPI by my fellow witnesses. They are added to a whole history of conflicts over land, which is the very history of Brazil for four centuries, the 'four centuries of the great landed estates' of Alberto Passos Guimaraes.

"Add up the six statements presented here by ecclesiastical representatives and an impressive chart of conflicts will take shape— and *only* for the geographical areas to which their statements refer."

He cites data, figures, numbers of conflicts, which add up to thousands. "There is a *history* here—it is not limited to today." Then he restricts his own statement "to the area of the northeast of Mato Grosso" and gives a short history of the starting points, which ends thus: "From 1961 on, the capitalists of the south of the country began to carry on their dealings in Mato Grosso with the objective of forming huge agricultural and livestock estates and the landowning monopoly system that is concentrated in the hands of big industries, businesses, and banks, national and multinational. . . .

"4) I, as well as the other bishops who have testified before this CPI, of course present first-hand information, heard from the lips of the victims and safeguarded in the archives of the respective churches.

"The tragedy exists, but it is not only undocumented publicly, it is unknown. Will this CPI be able to correct this serious omission? In the area of the three municipalities of Barra do Garças, Luciara, and São Félix do Araguaia, up to now there has not even been a union for agricultural workers.

"5) I must insist on one thing, although it may be disputed by those who cover up the root of the problem: this is not a matter of isolated cases. Thousands of isolated cases that follow one upon the other cease to be 'isolated.' It is not a matter of casual but of causal, structural, political conflicts.

"6) The constant factors in the declarations of this same CPI demonstrate this structural character of agrarian conflicts.

"These constants have their foundation in history, the old colonialist policy and the new capitalist policy:

"—with exportation and dependence, in the different cycles of the Brazilian economy;

"—with the compulsive creation of cheap manual labor, slave or semi-slave, a people torn from the land in a continuous flow of migration;

"—with the speculation and accumulation of land in the hands of a few, the mighty: the typical agrarian concentration;

"—with the old and new impact-programs and their financial incentives; banners one day, pioneer fronts the next."

The bishop closes his introduction with an extensive quotation from Professor João de Souza Martins, a sociologist, very critical, on the causes and consequences of the lack of agrarian reform.

He views the conflicts not as simple "isolated cases" but in a historical and critical perspective, and arrives at the conclusion that "the agrarian question is a political question."

The body of the accusations on the conflicts is divided into "disputes of landowners against homesteaders, disputes of landowner-managers against landowner-managers (the struggle of the great against the great), and the conflicts and problems brought on by the lack of legal protection in the lives of the landless workers."

In the final "Questionings," the bishop begins by attacking the current agrarian policy of the government, which violates the agreements of the sixth Interamerican Conference on Agrarian Reform, held in Guatemala in 1976: "The abolition of the huge estates as a socio-economic system, by means of profound and real agrarian reforms, is the appropriate solution for the Latin American agrarian problem."

Dom Pedro insists that "the structural cause of our blood-stained tragedy is the *huge estate*, colonial or capitalist." And he asks: "Is there a real desire for *agrarian reform* in official policy? What was the effective result of the letter and the spirit of the Land Statute on this point?" He then shows the contradictions and the futility of the promises of government ministers and agencies.

"What, to us as witnesses, characterizes the 'pioneer fronts' in Amazonia is:

"—The land accumulation and speculation by the few. Between 1960 and 1970, in Amazonia 44,000 small and medium-sized titled properties disappeared while 9,000 new huge-sized properties emerged.

"—Social relations of exploitation and semi-slavery.

"—Creation of new centers of instability, exclusion, and emigration. The government agencies CONTAG [*Confederação Nacional dos Trabalhadores na Agricultura,* National Confederation of Agricultural Workers] and INCRA [*Instituto Nacional de Colonização e Reforma Agrária,* National Institute for Colonization and Agrarian Reform] themselves are denouncing the situation of almost 11 million families without land or without enough land for survival. According to another official statistic, 30 million Brazilians are migrants from one State to another or from one city to another.

"—The cover-up of the lawless: gunmen, speculators. The daily violence. The violence and arbitrariness of the police. The constant interference of the military police in land disputes, thus breaking the law that forbids such interference.

"—The dependence on foreign countries. Amazonia has turned into a reservation for the multinationals.

"—Financial subsidies are given only to big enterprises. For example, the Suiá-Missu, of Liquigás, has an approved total of 257 million cruzeiros.[1] The Tamarkavy, of Silvio Santos, 54 million; Volkswagen, 140 million. The total subsidy to the fifteen forenamed estates adds up to 547 million. Each head of cattle on these fifteen estates is worth a subsidy of 1,568 cruzeiros.

"—And the unproductivity, even economic frustration, of the huge estate as we know it. 'The huge estate is uneconomical,' said a managing engineer in Santa Terezinha. Fifteen estates in our region occupy an area of 2,793,889 acres, and there is provision for the raising of 348,875 head of cattle, that is, 8.6 acres for each animal (data taken from projects approved by the *Superintendên-cia do Desenvolvimento da Amazônia]).* The San Antônio estate, near the Fontoura River, in the township of Luciara, according to the testimony of its manager, Raimundo Macial, has 72 head of cattle on 160,000 acres of land.

"Experience shows that family landholding is much more rational and profitable than the huge capitalistic estate."

The bishop asked why no subsidy was given to the small farmers, when one per cent of what is given in subsidies to the huge proprietors (who are already millionaires) would be enough to put in place all the substructure necessary for taking care of the needs of all the small farmers in Amazonia.

"Another question that we have already asked the authorities many times is: why is it thought that we must solve land problems only in cases of *acute* social tension? Real social tension is permanent misery, insecurity, unemployment. Any other kind of consideration is suspected of trying to silence public opinion. In justice, a few exceptions do not constitute a just order.

"It is necessary also to insist on the total truth of real solutions.

"Agrarian reform is not just distributing lands *but creating, together with the distributed lands, the necessary conditions* to cultivate them properly and to deal with the market. See what happens to the homesteader when, as in Santa Terezinha, he wins the land, but only the land; he is left an island in the ocean of huge financed landownership."

And he detailed circumstances and data that illustrated the moribund inferiority of the small farmers, even in the best of cases.

Toward the end of his discourse, after denouncing "the lack of control by the Ministry of Labor over working conditions of the landless landworkers, the lack of control over the destruction of the forests, the abuses of the police, shocking and well known, the impunity with which so many criminals operate," he asked:

"Why is every reaction of the homesteaders and peons who are defending their rights, and of those who stand by them out of sheer duty to conscience and the gospel, branded as *subversion* to be crushed by pitiless repression, with prison, interrogation, torture, intimidation and terror, expulsion, death? And why at the same time is there a cover-up of the violence of the big operators

toward the little ones and of the violence among the big operators? This is a simple defense of titled property and capitalistic
competition."

And the bishop of São Fēlix, before ending, permitted himself
this "homage":

"From this public hall I wish to pay homage to and express full
communion with all those who suffer for the *cause of the land*:
Indians or farmers or friends of the Indian and the farmer. And
especially my colleagues Dom Estevão and A. Alano, bishops of
Conceição and of Marabá, respectively, who have been summoned three times to military police interrogations, as well as
Father Mabone, who was tortured and slandered. To all the
fighters in that glorious subversion that consists in being on the
side of the poor and on the side of justice, like the Lord Jesus. One
day, the new Brazil that we are waiting for and working for will
rewrite with new words the whole history of this martyrdom of
the people and the church of the land."

In his petition he reaffirmed the need of a truly radical agrarian
reform, outlined six years ago in his pastoral letter *Uma Igreja da
Amazônia em conflicto com o latifúndio e a marginalização social* ("An Amazonian Church in Conflict with the Landed Estates
and with Social Marginalization"). He demanded reform of the
bureaucracy of the official land agencies. He stressed that "the
agrarian problem in Brazil is a political problem, structural,
causal." And he offered this bold suggestion: "Will the gentlemen
accept from me a serious proposal, although it may seem subversive to those interested in the maintenance of the established dis-
order? What we are in need of is not so much a CPI (Parliamentary Investigative Commission) on our agrarian system as a CPI
on our whole socio-politico-economic system."

"They'll Kill Me Standing Up"

When I arrived in Brazil and found Pedro in seclusion, writing
the new chapter of his "credo," he said to me: "I have the feeling
that they are allowing me to write my testament so that everything
will be clear."

I read the pages he had written and found many references to
death:

"Many dead, killed within the boundaries of the prelature. I don't know how to face this painful mystery."

"Fathers Rodolfo and João and the Indian Simão were murdered. Many similar things are happening in this country, specifically in this region, as also in all of Latin America."

"Latin American is passing through fire and blood."

"None of us feel very far from death at this hour."

"Since the death of João Bosco and as a result of other related happenings, I feel myself each day closer to the expected hour."

"Perhaps martyrdom is nearer than ever."

I told Pedro that God is going to upset his plans. "You'll live to be over ninety. You'll die a little old man in a wheelchair or in a soft bed, well attended." He laughed and recited to me that one about *"que te rondaré, morena"*. . . (I'll be courting you, dark one).

Joking aside, the tone of his writing and our exchange of ideas gave me a serious title for his new book in Spanish: *La muerte que da sentido a mi credo* [Death that Gives Meaning to My Creed] (Bilbao, 1977). And his poetic side was aroused and he wrote a few verses, with the Lorcan[2] title *Romancillo de la muerte* [Ballad of Death], reflecting what it means to Pedro to gamble his life here.

I know that Pedro lives in danger of death. I already knew it in 1971, when I read the testimony which Vicente Paulo de Oliveira, an employee of the Bordón Corporation, signed before a witness: "The foreman, Benedito Teodoro Soares, called 'Bôca Quente,' [Hot Mouth], on October 1st, asked me to kill Father Pedro and said that for killing him he would give me a thousand cruzeiros, a .38 revolver, and a passage to anywhere I wanted. And another time, on October 5th, he asked me again and again to kill Father Pedro; and if I told anyone about this, he'd kill me." I have come to know the danger with increasing certainty over the years, and I am convinced of it when I am on the scene. I also know that Pedro knows of this risk. And I know that he doesn't fear death, that he expects it, that he almost defies it. For him, death has been for many years his prayer, his poetry, and his prophecy. Now those deaths so cruel and heroic, the martyr-like deaths of Rodolfo, Simão, and João, the anonymous deaths of the peons riddled with bullets and thrown into the lake, and the daily deaths of the people, the death that surrounds and accompanies—friend, enemy, prostitute—the people of the backlands has brought to the surface his "vocation" to die for the kingdom of Jesus (could it perhaps be different, the vocation to live for that kingdom?).

At that day and hour, when night surrounds us here in Luciara, I want to know with no concealment, rudely, from his inner depths and by his own lips, what Pedro thinks, what he feels, what he hopes, what he despairs of death.

"You told me that the presence of death frees you from vanity, that it makes you feel yourself in the presence of the judge of your life. Since you arrived in these lands, beautiful but inhospitable, cruel to the poor, you have lived through very crude deaths, very violent, and very close. João, Rodolfo, the Indian Simão, and so many deaths of homesteaders and peons. All this must have branded your acute sense of death. Tell me, what have you felt? What do you feel? What do you see in the future?"

"You've known me for some time, and you know that for me death has always been a little like that song, 'I am the bridegroom of death.' I don't really know why. It seems to me that it's a little of everything. It may even be a question of temperament; that I leave to the psychiatrists. It seems to me that it's a bit of childhood experience. (As a child I saw those martyrs of the red zone, saw them with so much emotion, fear, terror.) It seems to me also that it's a little—so to speak—rooted in Spanish mysticism. And why not? It seems to me that it's to some degree a thanksgiving. I believe, with all gratitude and simplicity, that the Lord has given me this vocation. If some day I find that that vocation has not been fulfilled; if, as you threaten, I die at ninety-odd years and it is given to me to live, to be stretched out in a bed or on a couch, in any case, the presence of martyrdom in my life will have been, I believe, like a fabulous sacrament."

He slowed down, at the end of the sentence, to say slowly and solemnly, like a profession of faith, the last two words: "fab-u-lous sac-ra-ment." And he went on.

"Listen, all those famous meditations of ours about death, and the drastic books of Job, the sapiential books or the verses of Jorge Manrique,[3] and all our ascetics and the literature of death that we have read, I believe that it is all very insignificant beside a specific experience of martyrdom in which you discover a kind of vocation, an aspiration takes shape, a plea is made. Of course, you understand that this obliges one to be authentic, doesn't it? Look, when you dance with death, you have to dance well. You can't dance any other way. You learn, you try to catch the pace, to follow the rhythm—right?—and to become whole. And, in that sense, those deaths that I have been living, on the one hand have made me feel injustice in a drastic way. And from this has been born in me that passion for justice and liberty.

"I realize that I have never understood liberty until now. Honestly. It sounded to me like propaganda. I scorned it. But now I know that really 'liberty' is a regal word that is worthy of all respect. And it seems to me that in our holy church we have not yet created the theology of liberty. Liberation, yes, but about liberty I have seen no true theology. We might suggest to the theologians that they write it, if they want to add serious personal experiences to their science.

"So those experiences have given me that passion for justice and liberty, as they have given me also that holy anger (let's say 'holy' so that no one will be frightened) against capitalism, for example. More than that: against everything that is domination, colonialism, exploitation of one person by another. Now, on the other hand, the close experience of death has also roused hope in me. When you encounter so much death, so much stupid death, such powerful structures, deadly and indestructible, humanly indestructible, you have only one way out: to go upwards. And this automatically forces you to live in hope. It is related, of course: the more you live death, if you have faith, the more you live hope; and the more you live hope, the more you live death. Whether you are dealing with your own death, or with the deaths of other people. Because hope and death are for me a single reality. Because it is only in death that hope begins to be realized, doesn't it? And I believe that this and one's previous experience, the pathway that leads to it, must be felt as a single experience."

"How often have you felt yourself close to death?"

"I can isolate a few striking occasions, leaving aside the various dangers of accidents on the river, in the boat, and the many, many (almost an infinite number of) car trips in which we have already had several collisions. The first striking experience was in Serra

Nova, the town struggling against the Bordón plantation, of which, as I think I already told you, one of the principal owners is the famous creator of the 'Brazilian miracle,' the former secretary of commerce, now Brazilian ambassador to France, and whom some hope to see as the future governor of São Paulo. They were waiting there in ambush for me and Lulu, that likable homesteader who was already twice in jail, the leader of the town, the one you met the other day in São Félix. They were lying in wait for us. Lulu and I were on horseback, and Benedito 'Hot Mouth,' that legendary figure, gunman and contractor or foreman on this or that big farm, was waiting for us with some more gunmen, hidden up in some trees. But they let us go by. We reached the estate, after thirty-odd kilometers of riding, and the administrator received us ashen-faced, amazed to see us alive there right in front of him. We found out later, through companions of the gunmen, that they let us go by without really knowing why, no doubt because God willed it. They thought we would be finished off at the farm. That happened in October 1971. I was on a missionary trip in Serra Nova. Even the federal police confirmed later that that same Benedito 'Hot Mouth' had pleaded insistently and tried to hire an employee of the estate to kill me, offering him, as you know, a thousand cruzeiros, a .38 revolver, and a ticket to wherever he wanted to go.

"Then, much more recently, another significant moment was the death of the Jesuit João Bosco in Ribeirão Bonito, in October of 1976. He was murdered right next to me when he went with me to defend two women who were being tortured by the police in the little jail. Some people believe I was the target of that dum-dum bullet discharged point-blank at the forehead of Father João. It's possible. In any case, it seems that there were more reasons to kill me than to kill him, for he was just passing through the town. I certainly felt death very close at that hour, even physically, for he fell at my feet."

Pedro is wearing the shirt, white with wide blue stripes, that was stained with the blood of Father João. In São Félix he has, on his desk, the handkerchief with which he had covered his wound.

"I felt death very close a month before on the occasion of the death of Father Rodolfo, the missionary of the neighboring prelature, a good friend. Both of them, Rodolfo and João Bosco, were members of the CIMI [Indigenous Missionary Council] here in our regional episcopal conference. To underline these experiences, it happened that somebody, while we were taking the mortally wounded João Bosco to Goiânia, somebody who knew what he was talking about and had precise data told me that on the same day that they kidnapped the bishop of Nova Iguaçú, they were looking for me, to kill me, in São Félix. The informant knew clearly the day, the hour, and the individuals who arrived in São Félix. It just happened that that day I had gone to Porto Alegre, a village on the shores of the Tapirapé River. It was the eve of the feast of Our Lady of Liberation (the ancient Barcelonan Virgin of Mercy) and I was going to celebrate mass with the people. (Perhaps the Virgin freed me from that 'captivity' for the moment.)

"Besides, during the various attempts at expulsion and the various persecutions, with the Codeara Company in Santa Terezinha, or with the Bordón plantation in Serra Nova, or with the Frenova plantation, or the Piraguaçú in Porto Alegre, or in Ribeirão Bonito with various gunmen and land thieves—who simply take over a tract of land and then try to sell it—I have really felt death close to me many times. As I have felt it also at the tensest moments in the night, on certain trips along roads in wild country, in the forests, and facing certain types of persons, especially men in uniform or thugs. This has happened so often as to become familiar. Because in addition to my sensing danger, many persons have told me there actually is danger. Enemies and friends, companions, reporters, persons who have a critical vision of the circumstances. And really, given the atmosphere in which we live, it would be quite logical. One annoys a few people, or many, and here it's not so difficult to liquidate someone with a gunshot, with a fake accident, with a paid gunman, etc."

"Tell me, Pedro, is death haunting you or are you haunting death?"

He laughs a roguish laugh.

"Of course, death is haunting me. I told you so. And I believe I am realistic in assuring you that here death is within the logic of the system. The system translates death into action. Death is bought, sold, camouflaged, made official by all those forces, specifically here in this region, by the forces of the landed estates that exist also in the great industrial areas of the country; because everything is linked, is tied to the great multinationals. Now, giving an answer in depth to your question, I will say that, in this, as happens in love, I haunt her and she haunts me. How do I know if in this there is some kind of vocation, some kind of charism. You know that I have felt this since I was a child. Perhaps because, as I've told you, I lived in those famous days of the Spanish war with our martyrs of that time. I have asked for martyrdom many times, I have dreamed of it. As a child, as a seminarian, as a missionary, even, I keep asking for it. I tell you again: it may be an idiosyncrasy, at times I think that it might have deep Spanish roots, historical or mystical, but I think also that it can be a grace, why not?"

Of course, why not? But I press him more. "Can't you be exaggerating? The papers printed that accusation where Dom Sigaud blamed you for excesses that provoke violence. He even made you responsible for some deaths in the region, even that of João Bosco and of Rodolfo."

"We said something about this the other night, but I'll answer you. You already know that I have thought seriously about this at times, precisely because people have said it. Some newspaper also printed it, but it wasn't invented by reporters, they only reported it. I've thought about it because even some bishops have said it to me and some distant companions. Well, you know me. I don't believe it can be said that I am violent. I can be nervous, sharp, but violent? I have never handled a revolver, or any kind of gun. I have never killed a sparrow, and it hurts me to see a flower pulled to pieces. Now that circumstances here have made it necessary for me to speak, for me to confront the mighty, the violent; in that sense I may have been provocative, of course, why not? I believe that if there is something prophetic in one's life, it will always be more or less provocative; the Bible says this even of the very minor prophets. Moreover, it is absurd to say that I caused the death of João Bosco or Rodolfo or anyone else. It would be as absurd as to say that it was Christ himself who did it. Or not so absurd, because, really, all those who die for their brothers and sisters die because Christ died and because the Lord gave us the great touchstone of the new commandment: no one loves more than the one who is capable of giving his life for those whom he loves."

"Those men who have been killed here, João, Rodolfo, the Indian Simão, are they looked upon as martyrs by the people?"

"Oh, yes! Without any doubt. The people feel it and say it. They translate this into marvelous expressions: 'he died for us,' 'he is alive,' 'like Jesus.' The characteristic expression of the people is: 'he died like Jesus,' 'as Jesus said.' Even the episcopacy, which is more canonical now, has suggested the canonization of João Bosco, Rodolfo, of the Indian Simão, seriously, right in the full national assembly of the CNBB. Even though that business of canonizing or not canonizing concerns me very little (it even seems to me that the paths to true canonization are quite different), it strengthens my feeling that they are really martyrs, no doubt of it."

"Finally, for you, here and now, what do those deaths mean: the death of the people, your own death?"

"I would say that on the one hand death, those deaths, death present like this, in my life, in my people, seems senseless to me. But it is death just the same. I have never lost—not even when I ask for martyrdom—the sensitivity to death. Death continues to be for me the most serious thing in life. And yet it is senseless. There have been moments when I have almost despaired, and I have asked God why so many stupid deaths, apparently senseless deaths, because of hunger, because of distance, because of not having even a minimum of supportive structures, medical assistance, because of so much injustice, 'killed deaths,' as they say here, absurd deaths.

"On the other hand, of course, it is 'the Lord's Easter.' I have faith, I have hope. I've told you several times that here my hope has sharpened, has come to a point like a knife as I have been cutting the flesh of ever-present death. I can only have hope. No other possibility exists. How could I, as a believer, face so much death, in me, in the others, in poor persons, in the little ones, in the innocent, caused above all by injustice, if it weren't for hope? It is the Lord's Easter. Then it is death but it is also resurrection. I don't understand very well how, or at what cost to us, to the people and to me, but resurrection. I see that hope is as strong as it is blind.

"Well, now, I insist: it is to feel death and hope in me, yes, but, above all and much more, to feel them in my people. This is what has moved our group in São Félix and in many other churches in Brazil to make a decision, an absurd one for some, certainly risky, utopian, without much of a way out within the system in which we find ourselves and in the specific circumstances of repression and national and multinational economic power that the system has, a decision in favor of this remote country of the homesteaders and the landworkers condemned to be left without land and even to die physically or sociologically, to be shunted aside, as happens in the large cities in Brazil, in São Paulo, for example.

"And we have this feeling of collective and approaching death above all in the case of the Indians, the native peoples. You will be coming tomorrow with me to the Tapirapé and you will see the only Tapirapé people in existence in the world. The whole country, the whole nation, the whole Tapirapé humanity is there facing that marvelous lake, surrounded, hounded to death by those great landholding estates. As we said in the document that several of us bishops and missionaries signed and which was a trumpet call for the church and for the country, an appeal for attention, an 'urgent manifesto' as we said, the Indian must die facing the system and all the circumstances that the system unfolds, the Indian is a person condemned to death. I have felt this in a tragic way and there were moments when only through a willpower of truly supernatural utopia, of hope, can one lay plans for the Indians and work in the midst of the native peoples."

The machine recorded this dialogue with the same fidelity, automatic and cold, as other dialogues. In me it was recorded more sharply, and I know that tonight, and on many more nights, I shall hear echoing the voice of Pedro with the tone and force with which he spoke to me in this dialogue. . . .

It is raining. It is weeping in Luciara. We put off leaving until the sky clears. Some children splash naked in the mud; a cow roams along the street.

The door of the house and the windows, wide open, have curtains of water. This house where Teresa, Aninha, and Clelio give a kind welcome to all who come is like all the other houses of this poor neighborhood. Pedro told me that this decaying town of Luciara has its rich neighborhood and its poor neighborhoods. And on visiting it I could see that, in fact, in some ways, the differences are each entities unto themselves. "When we first arrived here, we stayed in a house in the rich quarter, with one of the first families. Fine people, of course, but, when we saw the true situation of the people and moved to the poorest quarter, they were somewhat annoyed."

It has stopped raining. With our bundles on our backs we head for the pier.

The last two images that I take away from Luciara are these: a dog in the throes of death, lying on the grass in a field near the river ("poisoned"), and Aninha, Teresa, and Clelio waving to us from the pier. Death and kindliness.

On the Araguaia it rains on us again. The sky, the riverbed, the banks are all river.

I find myself wrapped in a new yellow oilskin, sea-dog style, that my Cartagena friends sent to Salvador. Under the leaden sky, sunk in this immense gray river, it seems to me that I could be navigating at any latitude of the northern waters of Europe. Pedro, beside me, covered up in an old black raincoat and with drops of water on his glasses, brings me back to this kingdom of fire and death, to "this Araguaia, mute / as the people's grief, suppressed / as the people's rage."

The rainy weather helps me to concentrate and I reenter the circle of death so plainly seen, so clearly described. And I think how true are the many verses by Pedro that reflect that death, Pedro's death, the people's death, everybody's death.

The unjust death upon which they have raised—from which they have lowered—this Brazil of today: "splendid future of Brazil / established on the bones / of the peasants dead of malaria / fixed by the slaveholder's pistol / drained by hunger and lies."

The death that prowls in the region, and which I myself have seen, and to which Pedro, half-joking but seriously, has dedicated a "little ballad" that serves as an introduction to his new book:

> . . . You'll threaten me,
> I'll threaten you.

You to kill,
I to be born.
I'll threaten you,
you'll threaten me.
You with a death war,
I with a peace war.

You'll threaten me
or the poor of my town,
or the hungers of the living,
or the reckonings of the dead.

You'll threaten me with bullet,
You'll threaten me with night,
You'll threaten me with wing,
You'll threaten me with car.
You'll threaten me with bridge,
You'll threaten me with river,
abduction, accident,
torture, martyrdom. . . .

His *Profecía extrema* [Final Prophecy], which dates from 1968, continues to have the power of prophecy because it "threatens threatening death" and because it is the boldest and most serene, the most hope-filled statement that Pedro has made of feeling himself caught up by the Easter of Jesus, of living in communion with that "fabulous sacrament" that will be, to the very end, no matter what happens, the closeness to martyrdom in which he lives. It is one of Pedro's finest poems. In it the passion of his belief shows through with a force so serene that it is touching; it touches and shakes the reader. I can't resist quoting it in full:

I shall die standing like the trees.
(They will kill me standing up.)
The sun, like a major witness, will put its crimson
on my body doubly anointed,
and the rivers and the sea
will become the path for all my desires,
while the beloved forest will shake her treetops with joy.

I shall tell my words: I was not lying when I shouted to you.
God will tell my friends: "I testify
that he lived with you waiting for this day."

Suddenly, in death,
my life will become true.
At last I shall have loved!

Pedro lives absolutely sure that "to die is always to conquer /
since the day when / Someone died for everyone, like everyone, / killed, like many." That's why he closes his "Little Ballad of Death" with these verses that are like a song and profession of faith: "If we die with him / with him we shall live / (With
him I die in life, / for him I live in death.) / You will threaten
us, / but we will defeat you!"

I remember, like a bolt of lightning, the beautiful and brave
final prophecy of Pedro in his testimony before the CPI in Brasilia: "One day the new Brazil that we are hoping for and working
for will rewrite with new words the whole history of this martyrdom of the people and the church of the land." I give glory to God
that he grants to some the power of so much love.

The sun has now broken through the clouds, and this river becomes again the familiar Araguaia.

"The children bathing, joining the waters, like fishes."

"Today I contemplate the freedom of spirit of these Tapirapé Indians and their sense of community. I perceive their harmony with nature. . . . These Indians are all of them like one being, one family, one people."

5

Tapirapé: The Indians Must Not Die Out

___

The Poorest and the Freest

This certainly is the "kingdom of the waters"! Approaching a low hill covered with tall green trees, the Araguaia divides into two riverbeds, and on the left, mighty and dark, the Tapirapé River flows in. The Araguaia flows off to the right flanking the hill. And deep Lake Tapirapé hides on the left like a secret sea, small and tame, edged with forest. Above, on the hill, is the Indian village.

The welcome is festive, jubilant, with women and children greeting, laughing, shouting. The youngsters call to the bishop *"tiramuñas, tiramuñas!"*—"grandpa, grandpa!"

The men are not on the shore; at this hour of the morning they are working and hunting in the woods.

The Little Sisters of Jesus, who live in the village, are among the women and children.

Marcos, the village chief, comes up to us. In his arms he has a girl, abandoned by her forest-dwelling parents; the Indians have adopted her. She is now one more little Indian, happy, joyful, lively, with curly hair, much more talkative than little Indians of her age.

The hugs and greetings are relaxed, cordial, sprinkled with jokes and laughter.

The children didn't smile in Luciara, but the children and the grownups laugh openly in Tapirapé. In Luciara nobody has all their teeth after the age of twelve, but here you don't see one pitted tooth. "And there are no crazy people here," Pedro assures me. "There are no neurotic Indians."

We go up to the village. The Indians come and go, return from work, pass by loaded with huge palm baskets strapped to their heads. They are strong, as athletic as warriors, healthy, with beautiful bronzed bodies. Almost all of the men wear loincloths and the women dresses. On their arms and legs, they wear woven bracelets and hanging ribbons, *tamankurás*. ("Put on me a *tamankurá* of human dignity, / like a seal on my arms and my legs, / Mother Tapirapé, village mother, land still free, still human.")

The village offers me an unusual picture. The dwellings of mud and palm leaves, wide open, the fires smoking, and peaceful dogs at the doors. The surroundings, very green. The bodies naked, with happy faces and some festive ribbons. And the sun, like a god anointing so much beauty and so much life. "It is still the peace of paradise."

"And is this a condemned people?" I ask Pedro, who seems to me, among the Indians, to be another Tapirapé chief, a leader, a father-brother to everyone. Not because he is supplanting their own chief or their leaders. They like this bishop because he can understand them as they are, because he lives and suffers for their cause as for a sacred cause. "Are these the Indians who must die, whom you see threatened? Aren't the native peoples being made a priority in some Brazilian churches?"

"A good question," he replies. "They are being made a priority in some churches. I assure you that they are in *my* pastoral thinking. They are the first evangelical priority. For two reasons. First, because they are the poorest, as persons and as a people. I don't say they are the unhappiest! As persons and as a people they have hanging over them the most immediate death sentence, the most logical death from the point of view of the system. They are in the way. Their lands, their woods, their hunting, their marvelous territory, this Lake Tapirapé that you see, all are a stimulus, a lure for the greed of the great, of the powerful, of the landowners, of the highways, of national integration, of wretched development (and a curse on development in these deadly circumstances, right?), and of tourism. Because of this death sentence the Indians are the most evangelical cause. They are the poorest ones. Their survival is often only a question of months, two or three months—a highway that breaks through or goes by, that attacks the native organism that has no other reserves. Or a simple attack of measles can carry off a whole village.

"And in the second place, they are also the most evangelical in the sense that, by being the poorest, the smallest, the most unprotected, they are also the freest in spirit, the most community-minded, and the ones who live most harmoniously with nature, with the land, with the water, with the light, with the fauna and the flora. They make me think of the very ancient expression *Ad gentes* brought up to date; it always impresses me deeply. They are the 'seeds of the Word,' or rather, translating more precisely, 'the sown Word' is in these peoples. One really sees that the Word is sown here.

"Today I contemplate the freedom of spirit of these Tapirapé Indians and their sense of community. I perceive their harmony with nature. They are part of this earth, of the lake with its fishes and birds, of the sun and the moon, which are a part of them. They are the natural tourists, the pure ones, the authentic ones, the permanent ones recreated by and recreative of this beautiful mother nature.

"I observe that these Indians are all of them like one being, one family, one people. And each one belongs to all, even after dying, for the Tapirapé bury their dead at home, in the center of the tent, next to the main pole. 'If we always were together, we shall always be together.' They bury them wrapped in their own netting, in the hammocks in which they slept with the family, and they cover them with a roof of boards without touching their bodies. And the floor of the tent isn't flat as it was before; a mound of clay clearly indicates the presence of the one who goes on being in the family. I have seen buried even the little fetus of a miscarriage; I have seen the little bulge of clay, like a pregnant belly, touched by caresses at the center of the home.

"Certainly, 'the seeds of the Word,' 'the sown Word.'

"They could regenerate us all, and they are threatened by the greed of the big landowners, by 'dismal development,' by tourism, by the 'famous highways of national integration' ('Transbitterness' is what the Transamazonian Highway is called around here, even by the thirteen-year-old prostitutes).

In the environs of the Tapirapé village an old ship was converted into a luxurious Floating Hotel. We saw it close up, anchored next to an island in the Araguaia. The ultimate in pleasure and adventure, at a cost of one hundred to five hundred dollars a day. Its owner is German. For these Indians it's like an enemy warship, a destroyer, a threat. The prelature struggles to fend off the tourists, away from Lake Tapirapé, far from its waters. To change these Indians into a tourist attraction for bored multimillionaires, capricious invaders thirsty for strong exotic sensations, would be a most serious crime."

I ask him: "Does your defense of the Indians have any chance, or is it madness, a lost cause?"

"Look, to the extent that the church in Brazil, and the whole continental church, know how to and want to make the proper amends and to take up evangelically the cause of the Indians, they will really be a shock for the whole church and for our society, and for that very reason a most powerful evangelical force. But, of course, in order to take up in this way the cause of the natives, they must strip themselves of all pastoral ethnocentricity, of all colonialism. But really strip. A stripping that must be extremely lucid, even scientifically lucid, and perhaps heroic. Why not, if that implies abandoning many things, thinking in other ways, giving up a great deal, even giving up religion itself."

He has put a lot of emphasis on this last giving up. There is a silence.

"It's no longer simply giving up customs, ways of eating and dressing, or seeing and feeling. It's not even a question of giving up only philosophies. It's giving up even religion itself. I don't say giving up faith, of course. You understand me perfectly."

I continue: "Tell me about the present status of your struggle for the cause of the Indians. What steps have you all taken, what guarantees or what real possibilities do you have of making progress?"

"It would be well to start from a more global, more continental vision. There was first a colonialist phase that I am not going to describe here (we have history books for that), in which Father Las Casas[1] said great things and said them very well, right? This is a saint to whom I am devoted and to whom I would raise a monument—though that is not necessary—in every native village on the continent, and in front of every monastery of missionary friars, and in front of every cathedral so that their eyes would have to take in Las Casas, and the stone would remind them of his cry! He warned us in time. Only four centuries later does it seem that we have begun to awake. . . .

"Then, with an overview of the whole continent, we would have to point out a few figures in various places. In Mexico, Bishop Ruiz: Samuel Ruiz, who was secretary of the mission council of CELAM, an extraordinary figure who deserves much gratitude from the native peoples and from the church in Latin America. You could also point out figures from our own land, Father Meliá, a Catalan in Paraguay working with the Guaraní Indians, an anthropologist and missionary. And other missionary anthropologists, other missionary figures in various parts of Latin America who some years ago, starting with self-criticism, stripped off their religious prejudice, Latin, Roman, occidental, etc., and have been able to distinguish clearly between religion and faith, have absorbed the discoveries of anthropology, of ethnography, and have even overcome the neocolonialism that there was in the council and that has occurred in the post-council periods. Medellín itself, in practice, did not even think of the Indians; in spite of the clarity with which Medellín saw the continent and its major problems! And there are 30 million Indians in Latin America—including entire ethnic groups that are headed for extinction, with those roots and evangelical potentialities of which we were speaking.

"Several missionary centers in Latin America have overcome

those neocolonial attitudes. Here, in Brazil, it has occurred especially in conjunction with the CIMI, the Indigenous Missionary Council, which has been functioning as such for practically four and a half years. Its current president is Dom Tomás Balduino, dear friend and fellow bishop of Goiás Velho, who does his job very well and is often persecuted for that very reason. The CIMI has other dedicated members who devote their lives to the Indians and who have been persecuted. Several of them, and I also, have been forbidden, by the president of the FUNAI himself, to enter any Indian village in Brazil. Orders have even been given to police chiefs in the different villages that if we entered we should automatically be arrested.

"The CIMI has collected the whole legacy, past and present, especially present, of the ethnology and anthropology, which has ceased to be not only romantic and Rousseauistic, but has also ceased to be pro-European and pro-science, and has become much more human and more pragmatic in the best sense of the word. And it has jolted the consciousness of all the missionaries in native territories or in the villages here in Brazil. It has brought out very important publications (the CIMI bulletin itself is a historical monument), and it has already organized seven epochal meetings of Indian chiefs; not for four centuries had there been meetings of Indian chiefs. These meetings are bitterly opposed by the FUNAI [National Indian Foundation], by the landowners, and by the economic powers, because they know what it means to have the Indian chiefs meet; and the Indians have expressed it that way.

"The CIMI has also organized courses in indigenous pastoral training, theology, anthropology, mission history, everything referring to cultures, language courses; it has organized regional commissions; it has a permanent national council and assemblies. In the first national assembly of the CIMI, two years ago, in Goiãnia, the basic lines of this pastoral approach were drawn, and it's worth your while to become acquainted with it because it brings together in a very lucid way, very complete and very daring, what an indigenist pastoral approach must really be today, here, and the specific conditions in which we find ourselves.

"On the other hand, the CIMI, with its publications, with its meetings, with the daily testimony, even in the newspapers, about its missionaries and its martyrs (remember João Bosco, Rodolfo, the Indian Simão, here in this northern region of Mato Grosso), has shaken the national consciousness, and that of the anthropologists themselves, the *sertanistas* [specialists on contact with seldom-encountered Indian tribes living in the Brazilian backlands], the scholarly sectors of the country. Now we are having in Manaus the first indigenist meeting of the Panamazonian pastoral ministry and it may be of extraordinary importance if it manages to sound a clarion call to make up for that somewhat unforgivable neglect of Medellín, which forgot about the 30 million Indians in Latin America."

An Alternative of Humanity and the Gospel

Pedro talks with real passion about the Indian cause. "It is important to bring out that in politico-sociological terms, and in biblico-pastoral terms, the Indian, the Indian peoples, properly understood, on the one hand offer a new alternative to our capitalist society of consumption, and on the other hand force us to discover the Bible in its simplicity. And in both cases—in a marvelous concurrence in which the Bible would be blended with the new society, which would be much more evangelical, much simpler—and in which individuals would be much more in harmony with themselves and with nature, and with their fellow humans (among the Indians there are no neurotics, there are no insane), it seems to me that it would show the church the way to become incarnate in the people, a people with some of the characteristics of the Indian but lacking the peace and happiness of the Indian, and lacking even the sense of community that the Indian still has. Of course you will understand perfectly that I am not denying the roots of what theologians would call 'original sin' in the indigenous peoples. I have already told you that I am not Rousseauistic. I am simply comparing one society with another, and one way of living the gospel with another way, among the thousand possibilities that indigenous life provides.

" 'The thousand possibilities.' These Indian peoples have values for a beautiful alternative to our old, bored, sick, prostituted and prostitute capitalist society of consumption. The simple view of this Tapirapé people in the early afternoon gives you back what is best in humanity. The whole circular village, between the woods and the lake, is now the family home and workshop. The men play with their youngest children. Lying in hammocks or sitting on mats, they talk, laugh, repair their tools or create new things, while the fires still glow (all day long the fire glows in the tent, a sign of familiar human presence). Sitting on the ground, an Indian weaves, with great skill, a huge palm basket. Another polishes an oar of nitta wood. Another decorates his oar with black zigzag lines on the bright red of this Brazilian wood, using vegetable stains and a rustic brush. And Chief Marcos decorates the naked little body of the little jungle girl turned into an Indian: with speed and skill he traces on the little body many lines, straight, curved, circular, wavy, parallel, convergent, crossed. They stylize on the body the shape and the lines of some fish or bird of the region. Painting their bodies is an artistic creation and a rite. Then Marcos paints himself with the help of his wife. They are all artists, with an instinctive mastery of form, color, and line.

"If the tourists do not come, here there is no supply and demand, there is no haggling, no market, no private property, and art is just art, creation for disinterested daily use or for the fiesta. And everything is in common, all divided up, all summed up in the cooperative spirit of the village, which allows no unfairly unequal accumulation."

Pedro reveals to me the special sense of humor of these Indians. They are jokers, witty and festive. "I've already told you that there are no neurotic Indians." Their parties, always community affairs, always ritual yet lively and spontaneous, creative, symbolic, involve their organization and their relations, and accompany the stages of their lives. Just two days ago they finished the puberty rites of four boys who have become adults. They still have paintings on their bodies and a flower in one ear.

When the sun begins to go down, the men leave the children with the women and go back to work, to hunt, to fish. "Free feet. / Made from the touch of mother earth. / Living walking clay."

The girls and boys play or go off toward the lake. The women talk, grouped into circles. Sitting on the ground of a tent, a young mother holds in her arms the daughter that she bore only yesterday; she has within reach a jug containing a black mixture with which she disinfects her baby's umbilical cord.

The bright village is a commune of families that love nature, live it, work it, enjoy it. A discreet walk and you discover the whole spontaneous life of a people that grows in unity.

I ask Pedro: "Do you have any real hope of seeing realized your determination to preserve this beautiful alternative offered by the Indian peoples?"

"To be truthful, I'll say that at times I have almost none, or none at all. And many other times, a lot of hope. And, forcing hope a little more, I say yes. Especially if we manage to make the cause a continental cause. And make that beloved and always dormant church remember that one must not love generally but concretely, and that the pastoral ministry can never be a great theory, but must be a great incarnate love, committed, daring, confronting anything that needs to be confronted. If we truly achieve a continental pastoral ministry and consciousness, and even a continental federation of Indian peoples—and for that it seems to me important that there be broad support, incisive, almost spectacular in the best sense of the word—I believe that the indigenous peoples could be saved."

To Revive a People

There were forty Tapirapés left when the first Little Sisters of Jesus reached this village just twenty-five years ago. The people were dying out slowly, the whole Tapirapé genus was disappearing from the world. There are now nearly a hundred fifty and they are increasing with shared joy. Each child that is born to a family is born to the people. They are a people on the way up, they know it, you can see in their eyes their pride in being alive, and this makes more dramatic their struggle against the powers of extermination. They also know and are grateful for what the Little Sisters, supported by their continuous prayers, have done to prevent their extermination through these twenty-five years of presence, of respect, of discreet liberative encouragement, of sincere incarnation.

With the three Little Sisters that today make up the Tapirapé community (Genevieve and Elizabeth are veterans, and there is a new Brazilian young woman whose name, if my memory is not mistaken, is Juana), and with Eunice and Luis, a married couple in the prelature group, teaching here, we have been celebrating the silver "wedding" anniversary of the Little Sisters with the Tapirapé village. We caught fresh fish, *tucunaré*, from the Araguaia, and roasted them on live coals, the hungry dogs held back by Sister Genevieve; rice, lemonade, and very delicious bananas from the village, some of them fresh and others baked in the sun, rounded out the meal. Pedro is so fond of these bananas that the Indians jokingly call him "big monkey." And Pedro makes skillful use of the nickname, like a good Catalan, collecting more bananas and more laughs. He even dedicated a poem to bananas in the series "sister creatures," where he pays them this compliment: "Emergency solution. / Proletarians. / Vitamins of the poor." And he asks of God the Father: "Our daily bananas, / give us this day!"

Young Indian boys, a few young girls, and a naked old man look at us, smile to us, watch us, sitting with us inside or from the door or the window, for all are free to come in or not at all hours.

Eunice and Luis are young Brazilians who have dedicated their lives and their faith and their Christian hope to the service of the Tapirapé people. Buried—resurrected—here, when they arrived as members of the pastoral group of the prelature they were single. They fell in love, got married, and have stayed here. Their young son has very white skin and reddish-yellow hair but his name is Indian, Wampurá (they call him Wampú), and he grows up, plays, studies, and lives with the little Tapirapés, just like them, one of them, with no more clothes than the loincloth and cord around his waist, the *tamankurá* ribbons on his legs, and the necklace with its amulet around his neck. At the age of four he has survived several bouts with malaria, like any native, for the mosquitoes that transmit malaria are also creatures of this village.

Eunice and Luis teach and learn, extraordinary witnesses to the resurgence of this people. With their professional training, their sensitivity, their respect, their faith, their self-sacrificing and wholehearted dedication, they share in the conscientization and the cultural self-perservation of the Tapirapé people. They face enormous difficulties from official policies that oppose anything that promotes autonomy for the Indians, whom vested interests want to "integrate," uprooting them from their own culture. It is moving to consider the seriousness of the personal and joint choices of these young persons who, like their comrades who live and work in the other towns of the prelature, carry on their young bodies the signs of persecution and torture. They were arrested. They were subjected to questioning and torture in 1972, to make them confess the non-existent crimes that the military was fiercely determined to document in order to prove its thesis that the prelature team was really a group of camouflaged guerrilla fighters. When the two of them were freed, in spite of the terror and the tortures inflicted on them by the military, they came back. They came back openly to the prelature of São Félix. They came back to devote themselves to the struggle that perhaps has for them no visible future other than simply the struggle itself.

When nobody knew where Eunice and Luis were, arrested and dragged away from their territory, while they were taken from jail to jail, secretly, and were brutally interrogated and tortured, while they were praying and singing psalms in the cells of the military jails, from June to September of 1972, Pedro wrote "with much longing for the young fellow workers dispersed by the persecution" the poem "Absences," from which I quote, in loving homage to them and for other reasons, a few verses:

(The house has swelled with emptiness.
And the sun occupies the meaningless courtyard,
a little ashamed
to come in so freely.)

"Teresa,
Elmo,
Vaime,
Luis,
Where can you be?"

What democracy is that which persecutes you
for giving the flower of your years
to the service of the people?
What crime is it to be young?
What justice condemns you for giving yourselves without
greed?

What fear has been wakened in tyrants
by the joyous bugle cry of your testimony?
The waiting burns up the sun and the word.

(These verses appear in the accusatory document of Archbishop Sigaud as "proof" that Dom Pedro Casaldáliga is a "communist and subversive.")

The house of the Little Sisters is like that of the Indians: logs, clay, straw, and palm leaves. In a small space in the house they have the loveliest chapel that one can imagine, the only chapel that the Lord can want for his worship in this village. A Tapirapé chapel. The space is outlined by a thick Indian straw shutter; on the ground there are Tapirapé mats; on a beam hangs the Crucified; at the back, against a canopy of fine cloth that covers the central niche from top to bottom, a "jar" like a great red heart is the sanctuary, hanging between two plumes of brightly colored natural feathers; the lamp of the Most Holy is two logs gently glowing on the ground, clean, smoking like incense, the symbol of a familiar presence according to the custom of the Indians.

The Eucharist on this unique evening is an act of thanksgiving and thanks in action. Gratitude and commitment. Sitting on the ground, the sisters, Eunice and Luis, Pedro and I, filled with penitent simplicity and freedom, recall the problems of this village in the memory of the Lord. And these memories become words; we read the decree of the Indian Tupá and the evangelical text: "Thank you, Father, because you have hidden these things from the learned and prudent and you have revealed them to the little ones." And this word becomes for us promise, gift and commitment, invocation, song, thanksgiving, peace, and deep communion. Here everything acquires a new taste, everything takes on another meaning.

The sun is about to set on the other side of the lake. From the center of the village we see the shadow of the tall *takana*, or central house, the lofty and wide sacred tent reserved for the adult Tapirapé men, the pride of their architectural instinct. This *takana* is recently built. The previous one they burned last year in ritual homage to one of its main builders who had died.

I take Pedro to watch the sunset at the edge of the lake. Sitting at water level, we see the sun drop, enormous, red, and the waters burn, yellow, vermillion, purple, filled with light and mystery, brimming with life. The fish break the surface of the water catching insects and they create rings, hoops that widen and then disappear. Time disappears, stands still. Pedro and I, aglow with the glorious light and waters of this hour, reborn, reconciled to life, are silent. Only a somber verse of Pedro could capture this moment for me with "true words in the midst of abiding life." Here "I am the entire world. / All times are, with me, this hour / of sunset, upon the lake." Spectators of this unique hour, we have the feeling that when the day dies, death grows calm and the life of all things is transfigured.

An Indian dives into the sacred waters of the lake without violating its beauty. Indians are part of this kingdom. We, mere spectators, profaners with the grateful tremor of those who have been accepted, forgiven, descendants of other conquerors, penitent brothers of the white savages. They, the Tapirapé, are the lords of this realm.

At night, after an early supper, the whole village has gathered in the schoolyard. The children come, the women, the boys and girls, the men. Luis shows the film that he has taken of the building of the new *takana*. It's about the community undertaking that involved their cutting down and transporting the thick logs from the forest, their architecture, an almost choreographic and circuslike exhibition when the structure of the great tent was raised into the air. And it has something sacred about it, a ritual of community celebration. I don't know which to admire more, the skill and art that I've seen reflected in the film, or the fun and kidding that went on in the audience when different village members appeared on the screen. The savor lingers on of a people that knows how to work and create as a community and that knows how to view itself with humor.

When we came out of the school, the moon had also come out and had moved to the center of the village. It looked like a moon stuck up there specially for this Tapirapé night. On another night like this, Pedro sang of the phases that this moon goes through and the lights that it dresses in until it poses here turned into silver: "First it's born in the forest, red / as a flaming shield; / like a sun in embers for night vigils. / Then it becomes orange, and ancient gold, / and finally mother-of-pearl."

By the light of this moon the men of the village gather with Pedro. These meetings are always in the *takana*, but this moon deserves the courtesy of being enjoyed, outside, in the open air. And they, the Indians who do not use artificial light, deserve the courtesy of this moon.

Seated on the ground on big mats, they analyze their problems, the present status of their struggles to survive and organize, the steps already taken and the steps still to be taken, and they prepare a welcome for the chiefs of all the Indian peoples who are going to meet in this village in the near future. The leaders and Pedro guide the dialogue, which is spiced with jokes and laughter. Matos too gets into the conversation. I listen. And I also hear, intermittently, heavy slaps against mosquitoes on naked bodies.

After two hours of conversation, we retire. It is twelve o'clock. The village is entrusted to the silence and the moon.

This has been a day that for me is worth a lifetime.

The Rebellion of God and the Lament of Tupa

At three in the morning I get up from the hammock. "Net of poor dreams / cradle, bed, and shroud." I can't sleep. They've told me that the price of the hammock is an occasional sleepless night. There are no beds here. On my right Pedro sleeps "ploughed into the suspended furrow." On my left, Matos not only sleeps, he snores in the same key as the motor of his launch. We are only a few feet apart in the three hammocks, inside a small room in the house where Eunice and Luis live. They are sleeping with little Wampú in another room.

I go outside. The moon is hidden. The whole village is sleeping. I think it's not just the hammock, or Matos's motor, that won't let me sleep. It's that yesterday there was too much life for one day, a whole history, a whole people. And a feeling hammers at me incessantly: "This cannot die. The Indian must not die." I think it, I feel it, I hear it in the sacred silence of this sleeping village, without knowing if it amounts to a defiance, a commitment, or a lament.

What Pedro came to shout in verse is certainly a prophetic defiance and a commitment. Something like the rebellion of God facing the pharaohs who are blocking the path of this people:

I rain down tears and protests,
and I hear a voice crying in the backwoods:
"Prepare the way of the Lord, says the people.
Make way for his people, which is the people.
We have spoken!"

Make way for my people, which is the people, milords, says the
  Lord!
Move back your cows, have respect for them, for they are
  pure.
Pharaoh-Delfín Neto: "with permission" or without it!
I make way for my people, he says,
brimming with anger, the God of the humble ransomed ones.
I will part the Red Sea from all its bonds,
and I will dry up the Stock Market like a bed of cursed sand,
and my people will pass onward, treading dry-shod
on your programs of high economic development . . . !
The foot of a free man is worth more than an Empire, pharaohs!
I have spoken!
Put on me a *tumankurá* of human dignity,
like a seal on my arms and my legs,
mother Tapirapé, mother village, land still free, still human.

It is also challenge and commitment, the lament uttered by
Tupa, the Guaraní Indian chief, at the eighth assembly of indigenous chiefs and representatives, at the impressive ruins of San
Miguel, ancient center of Indian life. It is a lament of grief and a
summoning of all the Indian peoples to the struggle for survival
and emancipation:

"We who have lived through years and years of contact with the
civilization of the whites, we know only too well that the ones who
are truly interested in the life of the Indians, in the persons of the
Indians, are the Indians themselves. We have reached the limit: we
either advance or we surrender to the whites.

"My brothers and sisters, the hour has come to lift our voices
for the survival of our people who were in ancient times a happy
people, a people without worries. We are a people who had a native land and who no longer have one. We live in invaded lands
like intruders. Our laws are made by people from above who say
that we have rights. And we do have rights on paper, but what
happens in reality?

"I have a wound in my life, in my heart, that neither time nor
the centuries will close. For I am worried about my people. I was
trying to make summer come all by myself. But as the saying goes,

one swallow doesn't make a summer. The time has come to understand that by ourselves we shall do nothing, we shall achieve nothing. We need to join our arms and raise on high the voices of our ancestors who were massacred. We have come to the moment when we, the Indians, have to assume the command of indigenous governance, and this is the true road: the assembly, to gather together, everybody to listen to one another.

"Many times government officials put down on paper a pretty plan; they send it off and a report comes out: 'Oh, but the Indians here are very happy,' when in reality we're down to zero. I had an interview with the secretary of the interior, Rangel Reis. The Indians who insist a little are afraid of him, this is the truth. They told me that the secretary couldn't see me, but I waited. And I told the secretary that the trouble is that the new Indian law cannot be applied generally. That the Indian problem today is complicated, that there's a big difference between the problems of the Indians of the south and those of the northern Indians, in the Amazon. I said to him: 'See here, Mr. Secretary, this problem of the emancipation of the Indian is very premature.' Because emancipation, dearly beloved brothers and sisters, is based on the economic problem. If the Indians don't solve it, they can't be emancipated, they lack the means. Here is the beginning of our emancipation. So let us interlock our thoughts, our courage, because today we need to have much courage. Because there are some persons who appreciate the Indian, but there are many who want to exterminate the Indians so as to take the little that we have.

"There are nights when I can't sleep, thinking about our problems. We are tired of waiting. All of us here have the same experience. Our reservations are devastated, without wood. Who cut it down? Was it the Indian in order to build houses? No! It was the whites. We can't stay any longer with our arms crossed. This may be the last opportunity to raise the voices of our tribes. Outside there are very good people from the press and from television.

"The FUNAI didn't like to see the Indian being interviewed on television. They went and threw the Indian out the door of *Radio Nacional*. We must not be afraid. We are in our own country. We are in our native land. Our ancestors were born here, lived here. And the history of our people is a very long history. And so we have to cry out.

"Beloved brothers and sisters, now I feel happy here. I feel myself repaid by our meeting. I shall not be still any longer. I shall protest, I shall speak, I shall accuse. I already had a police captain, there in my village, who got together with the chief in charge in order to persecute the Indians. There was persecution. I was persecuted, my people were persecuted. They got together with the chief to enslave our people. They were arrested, tied with wire, taken off to the police station. The girls couldn't leave the house; they were arrested by the police set up against the Indians, taken to the captain's estate, stripped of their clothes, and jailed for the night. I suffered much. Once they beat me, they sentenced me, they sent me to Dourados. There I slept between soldiers as if I were a dangerous criminal. There I made my statement. When I arrived, the man in charge had sent my children, my wife, everything to Dourados; they had been expelled. I had lived there thirty years. Speaking frankly, it must be said that FUNAI has no people with the moral capacity or physical capacity to attend to anything. Some day maybe the Brazilian white people will know the true story of the Indians of Brazil.

"Do not be frightened, do not be discouraged. We are going to think of all the Indians, as a nation, so that in a not too distant future we will have the opportunity to see our tribes survive and be emancipated. To the man in charge, I said: 'You are one of the elements that took our happiness from us. That characteristic of the Indian that you call laziness is in reality happiness that the Indian brings from his past. Do you all believe that the person who lives that happiness is going to become accustomed to living with that toil and that hotheadedness with which you live?'

"I had been dreaming for a long time of an assembly of the Indians. This is marvelous. There are some who want us to go always with a yoke around our necks. I am moved and very grateful to you, especially to all of you who are interested in restoring our tribe, which was in the past a great nation."

"Bury Me in the Village of Light"

When day broke, sleep overcame me as if I had already passed my hammock apprenticeship.

There is a smell of toast and new-dawned grass. We devoured the delicious toast that Luis had prepared and we left.

The launch takes off, leaving the shore behind. On leaving the silvery waters of this lake and losing sight of the hill with the living figures of the Tapirapé in their "luminous village," the whole free human life of our Indian brothers and sisters, and the benevolent hope of Eunice and Luis (Wampú is hope personified) and of the most devoted contemplatives that I know, those Little Sisters of Jesus, weigh on our hearts with an immense nostalgia.

This is just the hour for the verse in which Pedro refuses to take leave of this village—mother Tapirapé—and vows to be sown in it forever.

> If I'm not killed by a bodyguard's pistol, on the road, far off
>   like a fleeing peasant,
> if the woods or the river don't bury me
> on their own account, under an *ipé* tree or between the white
>   ravines,
> bury me in the village of light,
> within your clay and your palm trees,
> Little Blue Sisters,
> or bury me in the shadowy house—head of the tribe—
> of the great Txankuianpani—
> the most friendly, most sensible, most unpretentiously noble
> of all the men that I have known—
> lying in a hammock of good cotton,
> planted and picked and combed and spun and woven
> by these Indian hands, creative,
> day after day (moon after moon, over all,
> when the wind does not disturb the gentle play of the cotton,
> and with the night,
> haste and progress are stilled;
> when God still walks about
> through this pure village
> before the time of sin . . .).

Sister Elizabeth, also an image of "before the time of sin," enjoys in the breeze, in the launch, the freedom of the waters and the birds. ("The birds are free when people are free.") The Little Sister comes to Santa Terezinha to get some injections in the dispensary, to obtain relief from the malaria that is attacking her. No one would believe this to see her smile as she greets the Carajá

Indians who watch us from the edge of their village, down the Araguaia, beyond the Tapirapé village. The itinerant Carajá of the river banks, tourists on the beautiful shores of the Araguaia. Another Indian people sentenced, but who must not die out.

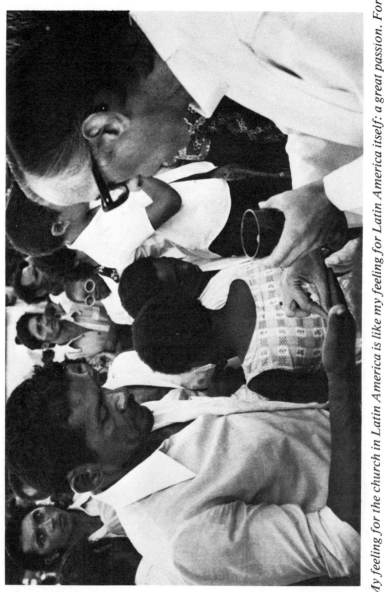

"My feeling for the church in Latin America is like my feeling for Latin America itself: a great passion. For that very reason, I feel extraordinary love, an immense hope, and some jealousy also."

6

Losses and Gains of the Church in Latin America

Pedro Freedom of Speech

"Again this unchangeable river / in its color of honey."

It's my last stop along the Araguaia. At Santa Terezinha I shall take leave of Pedro. He will return with Matos to São Félix in the launch, and I shall wait for the little twin-engined plane that flies as far as Brasilia. Before that, Pedro and I have several dialogues scheduled and a visit to this Santa Terezinha of the squabble with the invading Codeara Company, which cost Father François Jentel a false accusation, a trial, imprisonment, and expulsion to his native France.

Before heading toward the dock at Santa Terezinha, which is on an arm of the Araguaia, we glimpse on a sandy hill, exposed to the scourge of the sun and the winds, the ancient "Church of the Hill" and the old parish house, a relic left by the first missionaries who reached the region.

Some women washing clothes in the river when we land are the first to exchange greetings with us.

Leading up to the new parish house, seat of the prelature group, there is a long walk. Santa Terezinha has a structure that is somewhat complicated and varied. It has several centers of population isolated by the undulations of the terrain. A long district extends along the bank of the Araguaia (a stretch that the Codeara tried illegally to expropriate), with the square in the foreground, open to the river, and with the famous jail almost on the same bank. Then there is a nucleus of houses in back, below the green hill, among cultivated fields. And, like a curved dorsal spine of the town, the highway stretches out, skirting the hill and then reaching to the simple airport; it is a broad avenue of red earth and grass, bordered by houses with rustic gardens and by the cemetery, very wild, with its tombs under the grove.

Everything is shining. And at this hour, ten o'clock in the morning, the sun begins to be unbearable.

On the road, Pedro points out to me the supermarket operated by the cooperative of the town farmers (which functions in dangerous competition with the store of the great Codeara), the new church recently blessed, with its new color scheme of whitewash and natural wood, and the storehouse—the silos—for the rice of the cooperative. "Later we'll visit all of it."

In the parish house we find only the teacher of adult classes, with her two daughters. She is the only member of the group who doesn't work at this hour, because she gives night classes. She is now preparing dinner.

Inside the house there is a courtyard with bushes, the well, and a friendly corner to sit down to eat, or to drink lemon water, and to talk. . . .

"Let's talk about the church in Latin America, Pedro. Globally, how do you see it now? If that seems to you too broad a subject, let's make the question functional. Make a balance sheet for this hour. Fifteen years after Vatican II, ten years after Medellín, which are the most positive and the most negative aspects of the church in Latin America? Something like a reckoning, its losses and gains."

"Look, my feeling for the church in Latin America is like my feeling for Latin America itself: a great passion. For that very reason, I feel extraordinary love, an immense hope, and some jealousy also, right? I do not wish to seem pedantic, and if I seem to be . . . I can't help it. Of course, I would not want to be negative (I talk about hope over and over again), but, to be realistic, to be of even greater help to the cause of the church in Latin America, of the Bible here, on this continent which is now also my continent, I'll begin with the negative, with the 'losses.' I'm going to list, to enunciate a little, some aspects that seem negative to me. Let me get them in order."

He concentrates for a few seconds.

"First of all, it seems to me that we bishops ought to know how to take the blame, to admit that we have many failings. Many have had a strictly European training, and more specifically Roman, in the universities. They passed through the chancelleries, too, and they were made bishops. Many of them have not lived with the people, not even in their own towns, and they have taken as reference points and as models the scholars, the bishops whom they saw in Rome, in Germany, in Spain, in Italy. So the hierarchy in Latin America ought to resemble the mother hierarchy in every aspect. Latin America and all the colonized countries have been childlike, filial, vis-à-vis the maternal points of view of their origin and dependence. This is still a serious loss on the balance sheet of the Latin American church.

"It seems to me that there has also been a failing, on the part of the hierarchy and the clergy, on the part of the church in Latin America in general, in that it has not had enough esteem for *Latin American* thought. There has not been recognition of the natural likenesses and the natural differences. Of course, there is an explanation: Latin America is not only a continent of Indians, it is not even only a continent of racially mixed people, there are many ethnic Europeans who migrated to Brazil, to Argentina, etc., Italians, Spaniards, Portuguese, Germans, Poles, and the rest. All those who migrate to a 'minor' country consider themselves, from their ethnocentric concept of an immigrant, to have the right, the necessity, and the duty of socio-ethnic 'purity'—not to get contaminated with a lower level. And they feel it their duty to impose themselves, to dictate.

"It seems to me that this has occurred very frequently in the Latin American church; it has occurred in theology, in the pastoral ministry, in the liturgy. This has happened for various reasons—because of what I've just said and because in the hierarchy and in the clergy, and often in the theologians themselves, there has been a lack of creativity, of initiative. That's why I am indignant when, now, certain lordly theologians of Europe speak scornfully of the theologians of liberation. When at last there spring up among us some theologians with the capacity and desire to think for themselves, some European theologians come along and put up obstacles. It seems to me, frankly, that besides being unscientific, this is unfair, antievangelical.

"Besides, speaking theologically, what is the true theology? What is theology? Theology does not exist in itself or for itself, right? Theology is only an instrument, a translation of the unique word that is the gospel and the Spirit; the rest is very relative, isn't it? And in every theology there is an enormous weight of culture that, for that very reason, is very relative, in the sense that each people has to have 'its own' theology. That is more than evident. Well, you know this better than I, but frankly it irritates me that certain people behave like that, and that's why I reply to them."

It irritates him. And on saying so he has become a bit indignant.

"Well, but notice, on the side of the losses, on the negative side, a great lack of initiative and of creativity in the Latin American church. And notice, as something much more serious, that all the current attempts at reform and neoreform hide, under the guise of renewal, a new conformism, a new colonialism, a terrible restraint against genuinely Latin American creativity and initiative. They hide a poisonous denial of the identity and the peculiarities of Latin America, working together all too easily with the repressions that are killing Latin American life. There are hierarchies, bishops, and pastoral workers who ought to examine their consciences about these failings.

"It seems to me also that there was a serious failing at a moment when, through a new political awareness, through a new attitude of organization (evident also in political parties and trade unions), which affected the church (and very logically, for the church is the world evangelized, right?), there was an upsurge of new 'Catholic Action' groups, as they might be called, the Catholic Rural Youth Organization, and another for university students. . . just as there was an upsurge of new journals, new ferments. And the hierarchy of the church, and many, many priests and religious, and—I do not say the Vatican as such (I say this sincerely and sorrowfully)—but certain Vatican offices in close touch with those movements, that resurgence of life, could not understand it, could not go along with it, could not support it. And the movements aborted. That created (I'm talking about Brazil here, and about other countries in Latin America) a great scandal, a tremendous disappointment, for some marvelous figures among the laity of Latin America.

"It also seems to me a grave loss, and a continuing loss, and enormously negative, that Medellín has not been adopted."

He pauses for a moment and asks me: "Do you think it would be an exaggeration to say that Medellín has not been adopted?" And he doesn't even wait for my answer, for Pedro knows that it does not seem to me an exaggeration to say that Medellín has not been adopted, as long as one specifies that there are some individuals and groups that have adopted it irreversibly. There are whole peoples that have scarcely benefited from Medellín because the majority of the pastoral groups and most of the episcopal higherups—Latin American, Vatican, and of other influential nationalities, like the German—have not adopted it, have not digested it, and are fighting it. Pedro answers himself:

"Medellín, on the one hand, has remained very distant. On the other hand, it did not go beyond theoretical principles. Moreover—and this is the most tragic result—it has come to be a kind of gargoyle as if the best thing that could be done with it would be to touch it up, reform it, flee from it."

In an aside: "I am talking to you about episcopacies, in a block, and about certain hierarchies: you have been able to see certain episcopacies, certain hierarchies of Latin America, and you must have noted, for example, what certain elements in CELAM itself currently think."

I intervene. Pedro was going to pass on to another negative matter, but at the bottom of what he had just told me there is something murky that ought to be clarified. "Before this gets cold, Pedro: you speak of the Latin American Bishops' Conference, CELAM, of 'certain elements in CELAM itself,' with some anxiety. Tell me frankly what you think of CELAM and of its directioning under its present secretary, Bishop Alfonso López Trujillo, about whom I've been hearing all over Latin America, from Mexico to Montevideo."

He restrains himself. He has taken off his bifocals. With a nervous gesture he rubs his weary eyes. I know that he will eventually speak clearly, that he is not going to betray his sincerity, and that he will do so because of his passionate love for this Latin American church.

"I've already told you that I would not wish, just like that, to seem pedantic or negative. I would only wish to be honest and to make some contribution to the real good of the church. And so I must say that, from what I feel, see, read, from what I also hear from my fellow bishops and from others who think about and know about Latin America and its church, I have a rather negative impression of CELAM. The great figures of CELAM have seen their hour go by. They were the ones who really saw CELAM not as a controlling force, not as a kind of Vatican chancellery transported to Latin America, not as a Sacred Congregation for Latin America (with all the objections that one must normally raise about Sacred Congregations, because of their centralist and Vaticanist leanings, right?), but who saw it as a form of collegiality in the episcopacy and in the Latin American church, like a force that might strengthen the identity of this church here on the continent. That hour, those fine figures, have gone.

"And specifically, with regard to the leadership of the current secretary, I have serious reservations. On the one hand, I am sorry to say this, and on the other hand, I feel obliged to say it. I, and many others, have these reservations. I can tell you sincerely that in many sectors of the church in general, of the church that is most conscientious in pastoral work, of the church most committed to Latin America, even in many sectors of the hierarchy, and even in sectors that are not very advanced, CELAM has lost a great deal of prestige. I can refer you specifically to conservative sectors of the Brazilian episcopacy for whom CELAM is practically nonexistent; one more acronym, that's all. When we have our national assembly, we remember the name because some communiqué from CELAM arrives. And at the moment of decision, there are figures so enigmatic for one's thought and one's commitment . . . like the archbishop of Aracasú, Dom Luciano Duarte, responsible for the social arm of CELAM, when he is known here in Brazil as one of the most reactionary in this area, the episcopal figure most pro-government, that is to say, one of the most negative in socio-political change, even though he is very intelligent— one can unfortunately be both negative and intelligent. And with regard to the present secretary of CELAM, I tell you sincerely that he gives me the impression that he feels that he has the duty, the mission, to polish Medellín, to get beyond Medellín, to gild the pill of Medellín. Clearly, in this mission he feels himself supported by certain sectors of the Vatican. And he is intelligent, and he is very efficient. He can control, he can organize. I am even quite apprehensive about the coming Latin American episcopal assembly, if it is to be the assembly 'of' López Trujillo."[1]

I have verified that this is not a private opinion. It is a quite public opinion, in the church of Brazil as well as in other churches in Latin America. This same thing has already appeared several times in the Spanish press.

Pedro goes on enumerating losses of the Latin American church.

"There's one point that's related to everything I've said. At bottom, everything that's negative is fitted, it seems to me, inside a new neocolonial mentality, you know? They haven't been able to distinguish between religiosity and the religion of the people, as Eduardo Hoornaert would say; they haven't been able to assess the peoples' religion or religiosity, and we have forced the spirit of our peoples, we have disembodied them, and we have castrated them.

"A different subject would be that of us foreigners who live and work as pastors in the Latin American church. This has its negative side and it also has its positive side. Let's say that it has brought losses and also gains. And we must keep very much in mind that in Latin America, especially in certain areas, something occurs that has more impact than on other continents of the Third World: it's that we foreigners are of two kinds—those of us who come from another continent, and those who are from other

Latin American areas and regions much more advanced in economics, and with another type of culture. So then bishops, priests, religious—here we are foreigners from another continent or foreigners from another Latin American country. Of course, there is one basic aspect that it seems to me is ignored at times or is now considered to have been superseded: mission is and was and will continue to be 'mission.' I would never think of denying the possibility and the necessity and the requirement of doing missionary work, regardless of where one comes from. I have repeatedly said that for me nobody is a foreigner on this earth, and especially not in the church: any place, every place is my native land, above all in matters of faith and the gospel.

"Now, certainly, the enormous number of foreigners—bishops, religious, priests, nuns, lay persons—I believe has done great harm in certain ways to the church in Latin America. It has delayed the time for Latin America to discover its own identity and its own potentialities. It has prevented the coming forth of new ministries and new ministers. It has prevented one from perceiving the people's religion as something valid. It has often prevented creativity. And it has kept the church itself and the Latin American people in a state of childhood and, for that reason, in a state of dependency. And it has continued to be, consciously or unconsciously, a factor in colonialism and neocolonialism. We have always been a little like the cross and the sword, right?, the tents of the Lord and the caravels of the conquistadores, together, sponsoring and helping one another.

"Well, now, as I was telling you, the arrival of foreigners has also brought gains to Latin America. It is interesting to note that it has been certain foreigners who have contributed most to discovering that identity, to appraising the people's religion, to sensing the continent as a cause, to discovering the socio-political potentialities of the Bible in these situations, and to getting involved. One of these significant figures in Brazil was Comblin. Comblin was an indispensable figure behind the thinking and the activity of Dom Hélder and his church and his seminary. For this whole Brazilian church he has been a light, a stimulus, an asset of prophetic theology."

I ask: "The internal organization peculiar to religious, of so many religious congregations and institutes, may have complicated all that 'foreignness.' Has it been solved or does it continue to be a problem within a problem?"

"Of course, it seems as though there should have been a solution by now to intrareligious colonialism, convents, 'provinces,' and institutes and orders. It's high time, isn't it? Nevertheless it hasn't been solved yet. There are the famous 'enclaves,' and I don't know to what extent they can be justified in a truly missionary mentality and activity. It's one thing to have a congregation that has nobody here on the continent, and another thing to have so many institutes and congregations that have their own provinces within each country and continue to have their little enclaves, their small missionary colonies."

I rebaptize Pedro with the sobriquet "Word." Pedro Word. Because the word is certainly one of his charisms. He has abundance and quality of words. He speaks with the gift of improvisation. He speaks abundant and expressive words, graphic, incisive, penetrating. And he also has the gift of speaking with complete freedom. Speaking and writing. Those verses of his, so free and true: "And between Gospel and song / I suffer and say what I want. / If I shock, I first / burned my own heart / in the fire of this passion, / cross from its own wood. . . ."

Under the fire of persecution, at its cruelest point, Pedro asked his mother, in a beautiful poem, to baptize him again ("with the water of sobs and memory / with the fire of death and glory"), and to tell God and the world that she had given him the name "Pedro-Freedom." Well, I think that perhaps his true full name should be "Pedro-Freedom-of-Speech." From then on, for me, in this "continental" afternoon, that is his name.

Martyrdom and Identity of the Latin American Church

"What positive aspects have there been?" I ask. "What are the gains of today's church in Latin America?"

"The first enormous gain that I see, starting from my idiosyncrasy or from my grace (I don't know which), is martyrdom. There has been an abundance of heroism, of blood and prophecy, in Latin America. For specific names I can recall Héctor, I can recall Angelelli, I can recall my fellow countryman, Joan Alsina; I cannot forget the names of Rodolfo, João, the Indian Simão, so close to me; I can recall so many, many priests, religious, nuns, laypersons tortured, expelled, killed. And so many peoples (and this has been seldom said, very seldom realized), so many peoples that, like my people, our villages, have lived and are living in a state of persecution, in a state of torture, years on end, being really peoples martyred for the cause of the Bible. All those martyred communities that so much resemble the martyred communities of early Christianity, and that perhaps suffer under worse conditions from that point of view, with fewer possibilities of confronting the enemy, because today the problems are more complex than at that time when the Christian died only and clearly for Christ, only for the faith. Today it is easier to cover up certain martyr deaths and tortures by saying that it was because of politics, because of subversion; as if someone today could be a witness of the Bible in any other way. Well, then, I believe that all that the church in Latin America is suffering today becomes a force, a colossal evangelical gain, because I believe in the force and the evangelical value of blood; because I believe in the blood of Christ; because I believe in prophecy as being *the* strength of the church; because for me prophecy is the expression of the Spirit, of the storm of the Spirit of Pentecost. That is a gain that nobody can ignore and that nobody can offset.

"In the second place, another enormous gain, because it's in the majority, as it should be, and because it is root strength, are the base communities, *comunidades de base*. The base communities, overcoming all those bourgeois deficiencies of the grassroot communities of some places in Europe, that I myself have known in certain sectors, seem to me a community potential, human and ecclesial, which in future years will give Latin America a new face and a strength of testimony and prophecy, of renovation, and surely for the rest of the churches also, in communion with the churches of Africa and Asia, that church of the Third World.

"Next, and starting from that same strength of the base communities, the rediscovery of the people's religion is a colossal gain. The expression of the indigenous or Amerindian soul. The expression in music, in song, in the written word, including ballads, letters, celebrations. The famous 'mimeograph church' that we are living, because many times it's the only means of communication. All the expressions, very rich in popular religion, that make the peoples of Latin America refind themselves as a people, that allow them to express themselves as what they are and what they feel, make them authentic and make them communicative, and make them fermentative. For that very reason, it is an extraordinarily evangelical force.

"Another gain that also seems to me important, most important, is the new mentality and the new attitude of new missionaries. Whether in the interior of the country or on the coast. I call 'new missionaries' the ones who come with a new spirit, not that of colonialism, and come prepared. They are no longer the ones who weren't any good in Europe and who were therefore sent to baptize Indian babies and black babies and Asian babies, right? They are now coming more because of vocation, voluntarily. There were always some like that but now we've got rid of that 'blind obedience,' which it seems to me was very blind, and excessive, and besides castrating minds and wills, condemned the poor churches that received them to put up with dead weights or dislocated spirits revolting against themselves, against the institution itself. And the anger they brought with them they discharged here. Imagine what that meant! These new missionaries come with another mentality, with a new will and freedom, with a marvelous attitude, often, of continuous incarnation, meeting difficulties with heroism. The language problem, for example. I have encountered this difficulty, in spite of the fact that I have a certain gift of speech ('Pedro Word,' as you say), the spoken and written word. I sacrificed Catalan one day; here I have had to sacrifice Spanish. Of course you enrich yourself, clearly, but you also impoverish yourself in certain possibilities. As I said on some occasion, one never manages to achieve a perfect image in a second language. Many ethnocentricities are overcome, from language to the way of eating or dressing, or the music you sing or listen to, or the distances you live away from your family; and we ought to know how to live with a little more generosity, right?"

He looks at me in silence, and then continues:

"At this point, even parenthetically, let's go back to the losses, because that's where we are, in general, with a negative balance. I don't know why missionaries have to go back every three or every five years, like that, mathematically, systematically, to see the old country, and not even primarily to visit their parents—though one has, and ought to have, great filial affection. On the basis of a missionary incarnation, and above all an incarnation in the midst of the poor, I don't see how they can allow themselves such trips. I can't even see how all the immigrants here, in this America, can return every three or every five years to their original countries, and travel around three or four months in Spain and Italy. I don't understand it."

(Now the parenthesis is mine, to tell the reader that Pedro "doesn't understand" because he sees the matter very clearly from his own option and experience, situated very clearly in the most radical demands of the Bible. Pedro now "cannot" leave Brazil because he could not get back in. It would be his "expulsion." But before there was this danger, when he first came to Brazil ten years ago, his decision soon matured and he wrote to me: "I shall definitely not go back to Spain. I believe I shall never go, because I am poor and because I am the bishop of these people. None of my people could permit themselves a trip like that." Of course, this is his personal choice, following certain priority demands of the gospel. There are cases that Pedro understands very well.)

"There would be other gains, other positive aspects. All intertwined. As we were saying, just as the enemy is a single entity, so friends, new forces, are in the end reduced to a single one also: one used to deny the identity, now one discovers and lives it on the basis of the incarnation of the Bible in each place and in this time. That new gain to which I want to refer is in relation to the base communities, and it's because a new kind of lay person is coming to the fore. Movements, organizations, associations are declining, and we see the emergence of the secular church, just like that, in a much clearer, much more direct way. (Of course, this is occurring also in other parts of the world; it is clearly not a question of a phenomenon exclusive to us.) With this, the true new ministers are appearing, the true new ministries.

"I will say, in passing, that this has been a very grave concern of our little church of São Félix, and for that very reason we have no association, no movement, no ministry with special names, impositions, or solemnizations. When the measles of the ministries broke out, even in very good churches, very important ones here in Brazil, there was a great haste to create new ministries and to impose them, for example, the famous deacons. By doing so they created what came to be called the 'mini-priests.' The layman was clericalized again—and so many of them!—especially in the cities, for this is characteristic of urban pastorates; such figures of deacons, who really gave the sensation of being priests divided in two, because they were what they tried to be but couldn't be, what the others already tired of being. In short. . . .

"The true 'new' ministries are now being created with much more realism, at times without a name, without much solemnity and as a function of the specific service of each community and for the necessary time of service. I don't know why in the Holy Church we have wanted to eternalize everything so much, and it has seemed to us that you could be a priest only *in aeternum,* a deacon *in aeternum*, a minister of this *in aeternum* and a minister of that *in aeternum*. It seems to me that by dint of eternalizing things, we have temporalized (in the bad sense) more than was called for. Because we have lost the vivacity of the gospel and we have created classes, castes, privileges; we have removed the people from the people themselves. Those other new ministers were burdened with so many meetings that they caught 'meetingitis,' as we say here, acute meetingitis. There is a joke to the effect that, when the Lord returns, he may not find his church in union yet but he'll find it, no doubt, in a meeting. The laymen, ministers of this and that, were to attend I don't know how many meetings, national, diocesan, regional; and they had to prepare themselves in I don't know how many ways and manners, and they were kept away from wife and children and even from their own people.

"The newer lay minister to whom I am referring, who is coming forward much more incarnate, more from and with the base, seems to me an extraordinary gain. You know that I am almost fanatical—I believe sanely fanatical—about lay people. And may God forgive me and may my fellow priests pardon me the pedantry, but it seems to me that when we speak of lay people, we—bishops, priests, religious—ought to recognize that we haven't yet really recognized lay people. We are still 'accepting' them. And it still seems to us that we are conferring ecclesial rights on them, doesn't it? Because we have always confused greatly, far too greatly, the ecclesiastical with the ecclesial. In reality, I feel myself less and less ecclesiastical, on the one hand, and less and less removed from lay people, and so I feel myself more and more ecclesial. I feel of myself that I am a poor creature, a poor Christian who has a mission, which is service and sacrifice, neither more nor less. And what I say about myself I must say about the pope."

For the present, nothing more would come from Pedro. I am making him talk a lot and I recognize that I am creating in him a certain weariness. Nevertheless, I am interested in knowing, within this chapter of gains and losses of the church in Latin America, what he thinks about the theology of liberation. He replies:

"I've already told you that I interrelate all theologies. Because the more interrelated they are, the more effective they will be, because they will be more 'in the service of.' With this it seems to me that we shall avoid the return to the eternal and master philosophies, which for centuries, school after school, kept tying us up, preventing us from creating and thinking; the Spirit had to be Thomist or neo-Thomist or . . . .

"Interrelating this and all theologies, it seems to me that we must thank and praise the Lord for the birth of the theology of liberation! The first gain of the theology of liberation is its own existence. For the first time the church in Latin America has felt itself to be also a theologian. And with a theology *of its own*. This is a gesture of recognition and consideration of its own identity. Second gain: the theology of liberation has value through what it has of the strength of incarnation, of commitment to reality, and of return to the gospel, as also of the overcoming of dichotomies. The theology of liberation has been much criticized in Europe because it is considered to be politicized, excessively ideologized. Of course, this danger exists. I'll not deny it. In some sectors this has happened. But it seems to me also that it has helped to overcome the dichotomies that old Europe has always found it hard to overcome. Above all, our dear European colleagues who, with great frequency, you know, begging their pardon, think a lot and perhaps don't live so much, and above all think a lot for the others and don't live much with the others, particularly with the people. So it seems to me extremely important that, being the first theology that has been created in Latin America, it has committed itself to and has brought life to the Latin American church. It has, in addition, as I say, helped it to overcome dichotomies. And now, starting with that theology and from the commitment that it has created (of course, starting with the blood, starting with the Spirit), we are noticing in several regions of Latin America a return to contemplation in the liberators, in the revolutionaries of the church, and the search for the mysticism of liberation. It seems to me extremely important and it seems to me that it is a step toward synthesis, a true blessing from God upon our church.

"It also seems to me very important not to forget that, willingly or unwillingly, the priest-theologians of Europe have felt themselves a bit answered back by the theology of liberation. Although many of them looked down on it, although many of them believed that the theologians here were simple disciples of theirs who allowed themselves some liberties, I believe that it has helped them to think, it has responded to them, it has given them another dimension, it has helped some splendid theologians to rethink and to feel in another way."

From the austerity of this corner of the Mato Grosso, where lucidity is sharpened by the force of the conflicts, and where the gospel demands that it be the prophecy of the kingdom one hundred percent, with no mixing and with no compromises, I have seen the whole Latin American church in the words of one of its most radically evangelical witnesses.

"For me, the best thing about the Brazilian church at this time is that it is becoming a base-church. The 'church that is born from the dust by the Spirit,' as we like to call it, is already becoming a reality in this country."

7

In Brazil the Church Is Born of the People

Community Bases

We have crossed the wide street and have come to the home of Tadeu and Terezinha, a young couple of this group who traveled to Goiânia and São Paulo to take their little daughter for some medical examinations.

This house has its small garden in front, its entrance with a room on the left, the kitchen, the couple's bedroom, and in back a spacious courtyard with a well, the bathroom, and a shower. The house looks repainted and clean, but somewhat underfurnished, with nothing more than the essentials for simple living.

131

Here we are quite cool and calm. It is siesta time and in the street everything is fiery. I propose to Pedro a neighborly theme. "Within the Latin American church, what you know best is the church of Brazil. This church, perhaps through its development of life and prophecy with the people, is outstanding as one of the most creative in the world at this hour. It can be a stimulus to galvanize other churches to awake, begin to listen to the people, discover their own identity, and develop a greater prophetic creativity. Let's talk about this Brazilian church of yours. What do you think is the best thing about it?"

"For me, the best thing about the Brazilian church at this time is that it is becoming a base-church. The 'church that is born from the dust by the Spirit,' as we like to call it, is already becoming a reality in this country. It is even being persecuted, which is a good baptism, the baptism of blood. You know that Dom Sigaud himself asked for governmental intervention against the base communities. This church that is born from the people is truly born here and it seems to me that it is truly born from the people by the Spirit.

"There are many base communities of all kinds, of course; they're not all in the same line. But in most of the new churches (many of which are already dioceses, at least in intent, in programing, and in the commitment of their bishop, their priests, nuns, and lay people who are the most directly responsible pastoral workers), these base communities are really basic. Note that we are accustomed to measuring whether or not they are 'basic' by a series of criteria: first, if they are the base of a new church, and second, if they are at the base of the population on the poverty level. I also often say that more than base communities we need a community base, a new human-ecclesial community. This church that is born from the people is a reality. We have already had two national meetings, with very worthwhile exchanges and texts. We are preparing the third for 1978, somewhat larger, with contributions from the various regions because there will be regional meetings in advance. This meeting will be held in João Pessoa, where Dom José Pires is bishop, and also now, as auxiliary bishop, Dom Marcelo Carvalleira, who was the right arm of Dom Hélder Câmara. It's a very lively diocese, very successful, and very committed to the people in their land problems. In this popular involvement of the church, we have the company, the illumination, and the help of the best theologians, the best pastoralists, the best biblical scholars (above all, Carlos Mesters, a beloved figure, unique, very biblical himself), who have become interested in a committed way, who have even managed to live at the base, help with the work, criticize themselves, be present. For example, at the second meeting, in Victoria, there was a session so significantly ecumenical that we—theologians and priests and bishops—we listened and the people talked.

"I would go so far as to describe this phenomenon of the base communities as truly 'pentecostal.' Because it is basic, of the people, and because it is the base of a new church, it shakes up and commits everybody. And it's very significant that here in Brazil all the bishops (well, except for three or four) have accepted them. They even constitute an official program of the national conference of bishops. Although, here as in Europe, there are different sectors that have different conceptions of the base communities.

"These base communities (and I am still talking to you about what is for me the best thing about the church in Brazil) are generating new ministries. With this it seems to me that we are overcoming a hierarchical and clerical church, and we are moving toward a church that will really be 'God's people.' It is well to point out that the truth and the fact of God's people is translated perfectly into the base communities as such. And the suspicions that have been aroused in certain priests and in a few bishops are due to the fact that consciousness of the church as the people of God is still not yet alive, and there is still too much a sense of the church-hierarchy, or of the hierarchy with a people whom it directs, orients, teaches, and at times utilizes, and saves, and I don't know what else. Starting with the experience of the base communities, the new ministries come forward more spontaneously. There have been failures, there has been exaggeration, there have been reverses, as I was telling you, into certain kinds of clericalism, but it seems to me that, more and more, we are learning how to interrelate the ministries, to the extent that they are being considered more as services; they interrelate with regard to time, with regard to specific people, they become more and more community-minded, not only because the community chooses them but because the community as such takes them over, because this is how things are done in a community. This does not prevent or impede (of course, I am not going to be excessively utopian) that there are, as there once were and as there always will be, big leaders; that is only natural and indispensable in any kind of human community.

"Do you know one of the greatest effects the base communities are having through all this in the church?"

It is Pedro himself who asks me this and who answers me: "They are obliging priests and bishops to listen to the people and to sense the people's problems. And to live the tragedy of the people, of course. So they have brought about the interrelation of many theological affirmations, of canon law, of liturgy and the pastoral ministry. Listen: anybody who gets mixed up with the people gets contaminated by the people and therefore gets contaminated by freedom of spirit, by simplicity, by poverty, by realism, by commitment, and by communitarianism. That's obvious.

"Another improvement that those base communities bring us is that they are making possible a new image of the priest. As far as I'm concerned, this is inevitable. I sincerely believe that there will be the two types of priest, the celibate and the noncelibate. I don't see that the church is going to lose anything by this. On the contrary, I believe in celibacy, and I live it and I favor it, and I have absolute faith that, as there always have been, there always will be those who listen also to that word of the Spirit that is a charism, a grace, a service, a major availability. I also think, with Brother Mateus, for whose book on religious life I wrote a prologue, that celibacy may be *the* characteristic, perhaps even the exclusive characteristic, of religious life, because many others also lead lives of poverty much more radically than most of the religious communities (and this is already a fact in quite a few cases; for example, here, in our church of São Félix, the lay people of our groups lead such lives); and because many others also live obedience in the community in the service of the will of God, and of the church and of the world.

"I'll tell you more. If some new ministries have already come out of the base communities, and new priests will also come, I think that the new bishops will also come from the base communities. It seems to me that one thing will force the other. When there are different Christians, there will necessarily be different priests, and when there are different Christians and priests there will necessarily be different bishops. And we shall get to have those small, functional, flexible churches that don't need great structures or great curias, in which the bishop is the *episcopus*, overseer, a kind of supervisor in charity and in prophecy, who knows, who is known, who stimulates, who is committed and who commits, who coordinates with the priests themselves and with the other ministers, and who doesn't find himself, as so many bishops today find themselves, tangled in all kinds of directions, because the bishop is, in many dioceses of the world, the man most distant from his own church.

"Finally, to refer to another good result of the base communities that are part of that church born from the people, I shall say that they have demanded of us, and they are making possible for us, the rediscovery and revival of popular religion. I say religion and not religiosity. I was impressed by the position taken in this by Eduardo Hoornaert, who presided over a meeting of our whole prelature group: 'religiosity' is somewhat derogatory; it would be better to talk of popular religion in confrontation with the so-called Catholic religion (let no one be alarmed, he can distinguish perfectly between faith, theology, religion, religiosity; he is a sound theologian; let no one be alarmed). It seems to me that this road offers quite a few possibilities. I don't yet know how far we shall go, but I believe we can get quite far, in formulations of theology, though not in formulations of morality—note!—and certainly in liturgical formulations. This is evident, because, for example, a people whose popular religion is festival, is song, is movement and even dance, and is gyration (the famous 'gyrations of the Divine') and flags and flowers and lights and colors, is a people that transforms the liturgy; its liturgy, compared with our liturgies, our Roman liturgies, or with the spare liturgies of the new European church, is livelier and more popular. Each people is what it is, and in tropical countries, then, the liturgy has to be tropical also in many aspects, it has to be so.

"Summing up, let's say that in the lives of these base communities, the people is collectively a prophet, a prophet who denounces, announces, makes commitments, is a living sign. This has been very evident here in Brazil. You know that Brazil is a

country where one lives a religious eclecticism that is very characteristic, through native heritage, and above all, through African
heritage, from the slaves, who felt repressed in their religion and
who had to express it even by inventing dances, and who entered
or 'put on' Christianity, Catholicism, in a parallel way, as a 'cos-
tume' for what they were really living in their own souls. So those
new communities that are coming forth now are a prophecy. But
not the alienated prophecy that it used to be, and that it goes on
being now in many places, the pentecostal community and other
types of very spiritualistic religious experience, even somewhat
fanatical."

"Before I ask you for some specifics or some amplification,
why don't you finish or go on with your appraisal of the church in
Brazil?"

"What we call the 'sister churches' have been created. It was
felt that the south of Brazil was one world and the north (Amazonia, the Northeast, and so on) was another world. Even in specific
numbers simply of pastoral elements, not to mention money. And
then several southern churches made themselves 'sister churches'
of these poor churches in the north. The initiative came from Cas-
sias del Sur, in Rio Grande del Sur, where there is a very missionary bishop, very cordial, and where above all there is a group,
the very significant and famous center called COM, *Centro de
Orientação Missionária* [Center of Missionary Orientation],
which is and has been, with the help of God, in spite of many
persecutions, a historical force in the renewal of this country,
really. These sister churches help one another. There may perhaps
have been at the beginning a more or less paternalistic attitude,
but reality prevails, and those churches that came to help have
also been helped, and have been responded to. Now, in the national assembly of the CNBB, at the beginning of 1977 in Itaicí,
near São Paulo, as a basic topic for study, and consequently as a
program of the CNBB, the topic of the missionary regions was
adopted. And, within the missionary regions, the 'sister churches'
program, already having taken its first step, was adopted, in the
thought that there would be more region-with-region than
diocese-with-diocese cooperation. All paternalistic aspects had to
be subordinated to the conviction that it's a question of reciproc-
ity, in the full sense of the word. And the 'sister churches' were not
to extinguish the spirit proper to the other churches, their creativ-

ity; they were not to replace, but to supply the indispensable and awaken life. It seems to me very interesting, at least as a point of departure; let's see if we can carry it through.

"We also feel the necessity for making the missionary regions independent of foreign tutelage—not only in finances but also in personnel. We think that it must be the church of Brazil that more and more takes over the missionary regions of Brazil—without denying the nature of 'mission,' as I said before, which continues to be supranational. Moreover, we also aim to overcome another dependency within that dependency on foreign elements, the dependency on the religious orders and congregations in their negative aspects. A very significant investigation was made that revealed, with overwhelming data, how certain orders take possession of certain regions, of course, very 'generously,' the way many mothers act with so much generosity that they smother their child and never let it do anything. They saw what I had already seen in Africa and what has occurred in many mission territories: that duplicated structuring is an interference—the church, with its bishop, and the religious order or congregation, which always had more money, which always had more priests, more brothers and sisters, and even more possibilities of lay people working full-time, and that had more sympathy and many other things, but that was 'foreign,' was not the local church, and that easily created a parallel pastorate. This is happening now; in dioceses more or less neighboring ours this problem is felt, and it was taken up in a significant way at the last episcopal assembly. I believe that with this the church of Brazil is taking a decisive step."

The Teaching of the People

"There were probably other aspects," I volunteer. "But we can't stay talking here forever. Now, before closing this chapter on the church that in Brazil is born from the people, give me a couple of answers. You said that the people is a prophet who talks, denounces, teaches, involves bishops, priests. . . . We can then speak of a 'teaching of the people,' a prophetic teaching. Along what lines, in what elements, do you see that teaching of the people confine itself? In words, in life, in signs?"

"I should like to pick up an old expression and give life to it: we have always said that the voice of the people is the voice of God, right? We have always understood—rightly or wrongly—also that the prophet was speaking in the name of God, at a given moment, at a given hour, in a specific set of circumstances. And that the prophet was also talking *to* God in the name of the people, was shouting to God in the name of the people. In this sense it seems to me that the people is being the prophet of itself and the prophet of its own pastors. I have already told you that the closeness of pastors—bishops, priests, religious—to the people, and the fact that the people have taken part in our programs, in our evaluations, and in the reformulation of our pastoral plans, have forced us to be aware of the reality of the people. For me the first act of teaching and of prophecy has been just that: the tragic reality of the people, their poverty, their state of captivity; this has shaken the church and it will shake it even more. It is a marvelous prophecy that leads to incarnation. Afterwards it has also been a prophecy inasmuch as it is helping us a great deal to overcome the distinction that I was making between the ecclesiastical and the ecclesial. Where does the bishop end and where does the people begin? And the priests and the people? And the priests and the community? And the bishop and the community? In this also the people is a form of prophecy. As it is also a prophet through its own oral or written expressions, through its songs; marvelous songs are being created in the country, popular liturgies; through them the Spirit is revealed, so that we can overcome our self-sufficiency as pastors, bishops, and priests, too accustomed to distinguishing between the liturgical and the extra-liturgical, as if the people were nothing, trifles, but as soon as we reach the throne—great!—the Spirit begins to arrive. No. In this the people is a prophecy, showing us through the Spirit its strength and its presence, like Peter learning from the gentiles. It is curious to see how the songs and the texts that the people create are drawing away from those imitative and imported models.

"The identity of the people comes forth and is expressed, whether in land problems, in problems of food, wages; the wife comes out, the children come out, the day-to-day comes out in a much more normal way, and it shakes our faith and our lives, and prevents us from artificially living the liturgy, for example, and the pastoral ministry. Pamphlets and bulletins are being published. That 'church of the mimeograph' that I was talking to you about has a great deal of strength in Brazil. There are bulletins, like our humble and popular *Alvorada,* or *A Folha* of Nova Iguaçú, that are persecuted and have even been taken over, supplanted, misrepresented. There is in preparation, at the national level, a congress to study the phenomenon and the contents and significance of these pamphlets and bulletins. Also there are published small manuals, an expression of the people, as well as popular plays that put together and enrich the liturgy of the word. Of course, there are still people who are allergic to all that and who get scared. But I believe that this is an avalanche, a sea, of people and of Spirit, and that there is nobody who can stop it.

"Finally, I'll say to you that it seems to me that the people is being a prophet for us, the bishops and the clergy, because it forces us to distinguish clearly between the kingdom of God and the power of the world and the devil. As the people is being oppressed and suppressed by that power, we, the pastors, bishops, priests, religious, if we want to be more authentic and become incarnate in the people, we are obliged to feel that power too and to feel ourselves distant from it, and to prophesy as well. The prophetic spirit of the people stirs up in us too the prophetic spirit."

I ask him: "Would that be the origin of a certain prophetic language that runs through the documents of the bishops in Brazil in recent years?"

"Unquestionably. I have already said that prophets become prophets to the extent that they feel and live through the people and approach it on God's behalf, or on its behalf speak in the name of God to the power, to the oppressor. And it would be enough to follow, one by one, those bishops, their churches and their documents, to see that this is so. Hélder himself, Moacir himself, the church of Victoria, some churches of the Northeast, even regional churches, the published documents such as 'I Listened to the Cries of My People,' the West-Central document, the church of Goiás Velho, of which we have spoken several times, my document, my first pastoral letter, and everything that we have said. Whatever was prophetic came out of the contact that we had with the people. The harsh reality, the tragic reality of the people was forcing us, obliging us. The prophet's 'Woe is me if I do not cry out, if I do not speak!' There was no helping it. Notice even that the most prophetic document for me in the church of Brazil, *Comunicação pastoral ao povo de Deus* [Pastoral Message to the People of God], published by the representative commission of the bishops at the end of last year, came out, in its spirit, in its climate, even in its specific wording, because events were bursting: those deaths, those repressions, the virulence of National Security, etc."

"One critical question," I interject. "Let's dispense with the self-serving suspicions, which will always exist, in the face of this—to a certain extent—new posture of the church before the people and the people in the church, this church that is born from the people. Let's dispense with the self-serving suspicions, but let's take seriously the noble suspicions of those who may wonder if this isn't a new mythologization of the people and some new utilization of the people. Aren't some of you church people looking for a new supreme leader in the people, a new form of paternalism?"

"I would not agree that there is a danger of mythologization of the people. For me never; never, for all the centuries through which history runs, shall we give, either as church or as society, the value that we must give to the people. The people is the people, and that's that. Because it is the majority. And either we are at its service or we deny ourselves as church, as society, as intelligence, etc.

"Now, the 'utilization' of the people I certainly see as possible. It can occur. It does occur. And it will occur as it has occurred, starting from one ideology or starting from another. We can say that centuries will go by before we can compensate for the way the people has been used against the people itself and in favor of the powers of capital, of oligarchies. In that sense, there is little to fear. Now, it seems to me that to the extent that one lives with the people and one is in the people, through that power of prophecy of which we were speaking, you feel obliged to do a reevaluation of the people itself. With that it is no longer so easy to fall into utilization. Theoretically, it is. Practically, it seems to me that it will be less and less so. It is clear that in certain areas, like ours, certain works of substitution are necessary in the beginning, although they ought to be less and less so. You know that we have four lines or levels of work, and that for us everything now is, necessarily and uniquely, evangelization: matters of health, matters of education, land problems, can be, at this moment or that, a most urgent task, but it is substitution; we have no reason for 'replacing' society or permanently taking over the functions of the state. That *is* logical. There just possibly may be a danger—there *is* one—springing from a certain theory that I have often tried to condemn: we still continue to think of the church as a perfect society. For me, the church is not even a society. The church is the *ferment* of the new society that God wants. The church is light, it is salt, it is the seed in humanity. The only society that exists is human society. In that sense, to the extent that we understand that, it seems to me that we shall overcome utilization of the people."

It is mid-afternoon. The sun is still scorching the courtyard and the roofs. Sister Elizabeth appears, silent and timely, with some bananas and lemon water. We rest.

"*Conscientization and community formation are the two immediate objectives of our pastorate, in the light of faith and with the strength of hope.*"

8

Shepherd
of His People

Consecrated to Service and Sacrifice

With Pedro I have visited this town of Santa Terezinha, the
scene of the most violent struggles in the last ten years in the
conflict-filled prelature of São Félix. Here a war is being waged,
with some battles lost (the military sentence against Father Jentel
was overturned only on the second attempt, after he had spent a
year in jail and had lost his Brazilian residence permit), with some
battles won (the ownership of certain lands and their common use
by homesteaders; the health clinic, the cooperative), and with
some battles unresolved (technical assistance to the small
farmers; the ongoing struggle with the enemy of the people, the
powerful Codeara Company).

I have seen the homesteaders' rice silos, the cooperative that operates in stubborn competition with the Codeara stores, the new church, still shining in its wood and whitewash, spacious, very functional for the people and their celebrations, decorated with simplicity and popular art (paper flowers placed by some pious hand next to the sanctuary clash with Pedro's fondness for natural flowers and plants).

I went as far as the Morro hill, which is all sand but has enormous trees and a riot of shrubs rooted in its subsoil. "The old parish house of the Morro / is cooling, in the night palpitant with wind, / its ashes of blackened sand, / its blackened history . . . ." Old memories of Pedro who, when he arrived here in 1968, lived with his first companions on Morro, whose old church was the only one in town. Everything here has an aura of pilgrimage and conquest about it. The high stone walls guarded by eucalyptus trees, the green horizons and, submissive at our feet, the immense and legendary Araguaia.

I wandered around the "historic" sites of the struggle with the Codeara company. The health clinic that the people built and whose foundations and walls Codeara razed once with its armed forces. The townspeople resisted with musket fire when, weeks later, they came back to destroy the new foundations. I saw the low hill from whose dense overgrowth these people, outraged in their dignity and subsumed in their patience, welcomed with gunfire the Codeara forces that for the second time invaded the works with a tractor bristling with guns. There, right on the hill, in the jungle of the hill, the belligerent company invented a phantom street to prevent the construction of the people's health clinic. Then the company cut off the road that joins the town with the country, putting up a wall and screaming that the road was on land that belonged to it. At another time, the mighty one, to show that the entire road that follows the river belongs to it, set fire to some houses that were there, sowing terror; you can still see the traces of the fire, a kind of threat.

I crossed through these places with the feeling that I was walking on a battlefield. People from the town looked at me with suspicion (the climate is one of terror), believing that I was some kind of agent, but when I was walking with Dom Pedro they calmed down and opened up with greetings and fond embraces for their bishop. The bishop had to say to a few of them, "He's a good man, he's a friend, a brother from over there, from a country neighboring that of Father Francisco." All of them remember with great fondness the good, the peaceful "Father Francisco," whose expulsion is still an open wound.

Like Francisco, like Antônio and the whole group, the bishop of São Félix has invincible friends here, for the same reason that he has powerful enemies in the Codeara, which, in its hatred and power, manipulated military justice until it condemned Francisco to ten years in prison, accused of "subversion and armed violence." Francisco, with one year in jail and with his expulsion, paid for the just audacity of the people who, exposed to the aggressors, defended themselves and humbled the Codeara. The repression was brutal. The homesteaders fled, chased, persecuted by the military police, and stayed for whole weeks hidden in the forest, pursued like wild game. I have seen some of these men and I have understood their indescribable affection for and gratitude toward Bishop Pedro. They will never forget what he did to defend them, covering up their flight, encouraging them, bringing food to their hiding places, helping the women to harvest the rice that was in danger of spoiling if it wasn't gathered. "With a callous as a ring / monsignor was cutting rice. . . ." That was how Pedro described this experience in the verses of a poem *Canción de la hoz y el haz* [Song of the Sickle and the Sheath], setting the scene with this note: "Cutting the rice of the homesteaders of Santa Terezinha, persecuted by the government and the landowners."

These flashes, so popular and evangelical, of his pastoral style, show that the bishop of São Félix was not posturing when he changed the whole episcopal, or emblematic, symbolism for his consecration on October 23, 1977. He replaced the customary symbols and gestures, whose historical origin and significance reflect high lineage, power, and sanctified authority, with symbols, gestures, and words denoting service to the people according to the gospel of the liberating love of Jesus Christ, attested by the cross and by death. On the invitation-memento of his episcopal consecration he put this text:

Your mitre will be a rustic straw hat, the sun and the moonlight; the rainfall and the night dew, the look of the

poor people with whom you walk and the glorious look of
Christ, the Lord.

Your crosier will be the truth of the gospel and your people's confidence in you.

Your ring will be loyalty to the new alliance of God the
liberator, and loyalty to the people of this earth.

You will have no other shield than the strength of the hope
and freedom of the children of God, nor will you use any
other gloves than the service of love.

The preceding dialogues reveal the prophetic scope of the person and the pastoral activity of this bishop of São Félix, encom-
passed within the Mato Grosso in the prophetic lines of the church
of Brazil and of all Latin America. The present dialogue will col-
lect some of the characteristics of the pastoral style of Pedro Casaldáliga, shepherd of his people.

To Conscientize and to Form a Community

"Since your consecration as bishop, after several years of analysis, reflection, programs, revisions, problems, persecutions, and
conflicts experienced in all their intensity in this Mato Grosso,
along what lines do you concentrate your pastoral mission?"

"I would say that the ten years have had their private life and
their public life. In the first two or three years there was mainly a
sense of fright at all the diverse forms of *distance,* estrangement,
that I encountered, and I lived with the urgent need to get to know
and to feel reality. Afterwards, starting with that need to experience reality, that desire to experience incarnation, I gradually
defined our work on four levels that might be formulated this
way: First, the direct pastoral ministry. Second, attention to matters of education, on various levels and aspects—formal, infor-
mal, adults, young people, children, the different clubs, meetings, encounters that have to do with education. Third, health:
attention to sanitation and hygiene, in various aspects, giving pri-
macy to preventive medicine and health consciousness. And, at
the fourth level, land problems: to discover, to show, to illustrate
rights. To strengthen the struggle of a people for their rights; a
backwoods people, an Indian people for whom land is a vital and

basic problem. You know that starting from this struggle there arose the CPT [Commission on the Rural Ministry]—at the level of the national episcopal conference—which today in Brazil is, for me, the great force of renewal, really from the base, together with the CIMI [Indigenous Missionary Council] and with whatever we can channel from a specifically labor ministry, and something more generic, like the base communities. I would like to state specifically, with heavy emphasis, that those four lines or strata of our pastorate are, for the church of São Félix, a single evangelization of a single reality. Starting with faith and with the very experience of this human reality, we seek to conscientize and we seek to form the community. Conscientization and community formation are the two immediate objectives of our pastorate, in the light of faith and with the strength of hope, which clarify and consolidate and afterwards we celebrate."

"How do you make pastoral visits to your people?"

"You have seen them. We don't have that programed pastoral visit which, in an official way, at times with a certain pomposity and solemnity, at times with superficiality and distance, takes place in so many dioceses in the world. I try to multiply the visits so that they are not an act but an attitude, and almost a permanent occupation. And I visit every house. I talk with everyone, absolutely everyone. And we talk about everybody and everything, realities, joys, problems. . . ."

I have seen it, yes. I am seeing it. The trip that Pedro takes with me is also a pastoral visit. I have witnessed the directness and the warmth with which the people and the bishop treat each other. There is mutual interest—he in them, they in him—with absolute human-Christian normality. And the encounters, family to family, person to person, occur spontaneously, in the homes as well as in the street or at work.

"We always have some special celebration with the people and other smaller and more specific meetings with the town leaders. With the local prelature teams we go over everything completely and we analyze the specific problems. The bishop's most important work is with the teams; their members are the ones who do the important work. We have decided that the few confirmations we have are to be presided over by the bishop (whose contact with all the people in the town is, moreover, frequent, as I have told you and as you can verify), in order to emphasize that it's a question of a true 'confirmation' of their baptism, by means of which the Christian becomes an adult and rises up to the church and its mission."

"How many teams and people work in the prelature?"

Pedro puts his glasses on the old green wooden table and rubs his eyes a little while he goes on talking. He asks the help of Irene and Edina, who fill in data he omits, and he enumerates:

"The order in which I quote places and persons has no special meaning. Santo Antônio has only Sister Judit, who lives in the home of a backwoodsman and is the animator of the community and the school, and watches over land problems. She, like several others of other teams, belongs to the Sisters of Saint Joseph, an institution of French origin. In Serra Nova is the married couple Alita and Eugenio, who are everything: promoters, nurses, teachers, even shoemakers. In São Félix, which is the central seat of the prelature, with me (and they are there more than I am, since I try to be in all the towns) are Pedrito, a Claretian priest from Navarre, who, besides being the permanent pastor of the town, is carpenter, mason, and the architect and master builder of the new house and the cathedral, and he is a farmer and I don't know how many other things; and there is Sister Irene, from San José, administrator of the prelature, promoter of the community and the education of women; and Sister Cecilia, of the Divine Providence, teacher of adult education and the advancement of women; she is also an excellent cook and she uses her artistic hands to create huge pictures with colored feathers gathered locally. Vera is our social assistant and she also teaches. Zé and Isabel Wilson with their little baby Zelia are licensed teachers. In Pontinópolis there are two married couples, Pontin and Selme, who have two children, and Elio and Betty, with two others. Pontin is the promoter of the community and the backwoods area, and in charge of land problems. The other three are all licensed teachers. In Porto Alegre we have Maxi, the young Claretian from Cartagena, who is the parish priest; Sister Mercedes, from San José, a nurse; Francisca, a Canadian nurse; and Altair and Lucia, married (she is from Porto Alegre), both of them teachers, and he a community promoter and in charge of land problems. In Canabrava, Dirceo is everything: teacher, animator, counsellor. Ribeirão

Bonito, site of the martyrdom of Father João Bosco, has Manuel as priest, a Claretian, my companion from the very beginnings; then there are Sisters Beatriz and Magdalena, of the Divine Providence, the first a nurse and the other a social aide, promoter of the community; Juárez is a teacher, community promoter, in charge of land problems, social training, and getting the farmers together; Susana, his fiancée, is a writer and teacher; and Mario is a teacher, representative of the teachers and of the backwoods communities. In Santa Terezinha, as you see, is Antônio Canuto, a Brazilian, who besides being a priest, is a farmer engaged in the hardest work, the *mutirão* or community work on the land; Edina and Irene are Sisters of Saint Joseph, the first is a teacher and the second a promoter of the teaching of Christian doctrine, both nurses in the people's health cooperative in the clinic; Tadeu and Terezinha, a married couple with one little girl, whom you met in Goiãnia, are managers of the cooperative, and Tadeu is also a teacher; and that adult teacher and community promoter whom you saw when you arrived, with her two daughters. The rest of the teams you also know: Tapirapé has, in the community of the Little Sisters of Jesus, Elisabeth, Marie-Batista, Genevieve, and Juana; Luis and Eunice are the bilingual teachers, the parents of Wampú. In Luciara, Clelio is the priest and the carpenter, Teresa is the adult teacher and community promoter, Aninha is a sociologist and community promoter in the backwoods, and the horse on which Aninha travels into the backwoods (remember that as a child she lost an arm) is called 'Bem feito' [Well Done]. In Goiãnia, Leo, a Spanish Claretian, is the bridgehead with the whole Brazilian church. Naturally, each center, each team is created on site and it works according to the problems and needs of each locality."

"How do you coordinate the work of all the teams?"

"I have come to believe in the necessity of being a presence, of knowing and being known by the people and the teams. Everything that the teams think and do—to know about it, to think about it, to review it, to support it, to make of it joint participation. And to bring them joy, to create a real climate of joy, of faith, of hope, of fortitude. To bring them also the life of the other churches, to prevent their closing in upon themselves. To be a kind of 'coordinator.' To give ecclesiality through the person and communicative presence of the bishop. We have no presbyterial or pastoral council, just as we have no curia. We function with a co-responsibility more lively, more total, more dynamic and less bureaucratic. In addition, the teams have a great personality, and they program and evaluate very responsibly, and I try to be with them as much as possible. All of us pastoral workers make joint decisions about our actions: bishops, priests, religious, and lay persons. And when there is voting, all votes have the same value: the bishop's vote has the same weight as that of any lay person. All team members have two general meetings a year, which usually last a week apiece, with planning, study, and programing. They are usually very demanding meetings; most of the team members are young people, who tend to be hypercritical, and that is excellent.

"Apart from those meetings of all the teams, we have assemblies with full participation by the townspeople. We have an annual assembly by regions, with representatives of local communities up to a total of fifty, and a general assembly that seems to us a very important element because it brings together people from all the scattered towns. The representatives chosen by the regions attend, a subject is planned, and they are truly 'assemblies' in the most convocative and communitary sense of the word. They are not meetings for study but for 'encounter' in a very familiar climate, poor and simple. This year we are having the meeting in Ribeirão Bonito under the motto 'to build the church of Jesus Christ.' At the same time that we delve into and live the evangelical scope of the expression, we will build with our own hands a simple church for the town, which we wanted to erect at the very spot where Father João Bosco was assassinated, a thing that the government did not allow.

"Finally, in the coordination and intercommunication of the prelature, written communication has its importance through our bulletin *Alvorada*. It is a monthly. Four teams have mimeograph machines. We turn out pages and pages of religious and educational expression and communication. From time to time I write letters that are countersigned in a given color, and so, when persecution builds up and repression is especially unjust and watchful, the people know what their bishop is writing."

Frontier Experience of Religious Life

For several years I have been interested in the experience of religious life that the church of São Félix has been carrying forward in the teams that Pedro has described, within the whole pastoral process, with evangelical realism shared with the people. They are "mixed" religious communities, ecclesiastically speaking. That is to say, it's not just a question of mixing both sexes but of complementing functions, services, and personal options added up for the common good: priests, nuns, and lay persons sharing life and action in fellowship; poverty, charity, and struggle in a plurality of functions and of levels of commitments and options.

I talk about this with Pedro. About the contribution that this experience can mean for new forms of religious life in the church. About the risks that are involved in adopting this kind of experience, and about the risks that are involved in not adopting it. And about how dangerous it is to do this artificially, as a laboratory experiment or as a training program, from purely psychological urgings. And I ask Pedro for his authorized version of the experiment.

"It would be necessary to polish this a good deal, to color it right. More than time and space allow us here and now, and more than is permitted by this kind of spontaneous dialogue. Look, for me religious life would have to change a good deal. Religious life ought to overcome, more and more radically, its provincialisms, and the whole structural form that we keep maintaining, apparently as untouchable, which, apart from the inconveniences that it brings and maintains within religious life itself, creates a parallelism with the diocesan churches, makes for a kind of religious church, 'jealously' carried on, watched and watchful, and with the additional complication of always being the good example. . . . Religious life must be more and more assimilated to the local church, to the diocesan and particular churches.

"In the second place, through experiences such as this one we are having here, and even of others simpler and more common, we will get to see that only with difficulty can the poverty-chastity-obedience trilogy be justified as essential and exclusive to religious life. Celibacy tied to poverty and obedience may be very specific to religious life, but to a poverty and an obedience very closely shared with the forms of poverty and obedience that are lived by certain groups of lay people, single and married, and in close relation to the people. They, the lay people and the common people, live a poverty more bitter and more real than ours, less programed and less deceitful. And they have a sense of obedience much more fraternal, more community-oriented, and for that very reason more collegial, more Christian, more evangelical, less managerial and less paternalistic, because it places less responsibility on one person only or on one person together with a council (a managerial and political formula).

"Well, now, I continue to think that, because of the celibacy commitment, the religious, man or woman, must be a person especially at the disposition of the church and the world for the kingdom, and especially 'open' to all brothers and sisters. They will always make a gift of their person, of their time, of their things and their life, that the lay person who is a husband, a wife, a mother, a father, an engaged man or woman cannot make. The religious will always be to some degree the father, the mother, the brother, the sister, the husband, the wife of everyone for the kingdom.

"I also think that the religious ought to be, and must continue to be, a witness to prayer. If for some it seems that we've gone 'beyond' that, then it must be retrieved. Religious must be not only the standing army of prayer but also the 'witnesses': one must see and hear, and by this I mean that it is a question of very evangelical prayer, very committed to human reality, to the people. Prayer is also in need of a great reform in religious life.

"And, coming to the 'forms' of religious life, you can see that here we have no religious community that is 'separate,' autonomous, merely parallel to the other members of each team. The only ones who live in separate houses are the married ones and their children who are still young. The pluralism of our communities, as you well said, is not limited to pluralism of sex but is extended to pluralism of options, attitudes, services. Through this pluralism, religious would also have the opportunity and the responsibility to be more personal in their testimony and in their prayer, in their celibacy and availability, and they must be able to integrate all the values of their 'identity.' This identity must not be lost but must be purified and enriched, making its essential values prevail. Unfortunately, most of the time the identity of religious life rests on accidental and relative things, and so it is lost the moment the religious come into contact with down-to-earth reality. Here it is a question of cultivating and reevaluating all the essential values of its identity in the act of group life, renouncing what come to be advantages camouflaged under a kind of intimacy, silence, separation, confinement, for example, with separate buildings, separate rooms, call bells, porters, etc. Here our communities are 'mixed' through the integration of identities and the values of their charisms, and very much in tune with the demands of 'mission.' And this itself shows that it's not true that it has to be like this everywhere. And that in no way should this be sought for artificially, like a laboratory experiment, as you were saying. Our case is being looked at by theologians as a frontier experience, with all the benefits and all the risks peculiar to the frontier."

Night is falling. It is suppertime. The various members of this Santa Terezinha team have been returning home, one by one. Sister Irene has returned from the clinic and Sister Edina from her classes. Father Antônio has come back from his full day of farming in the community area. With him these days is a boy, they say somewhat unbalanced, who has come here to acquire work experience. He rubs the calluses on his hands and talks with Antônio about how hard today's work was. They are both red, sunburned, but look relaxed after a bath.

Here the bath at sunset, before supper, is a necessary daily relief. (They say 'to take a bath' although what they take is a shower. The shower systems here go from the most rudimentary—taking a pail of water from the well, carrying it away, and spilling it over oneself—to the normal shower. Midway is the system used here at Santa Terezinha, which includes the preparatory hundred and twenty crankings to bring up from the well enough water so you won't be left all soapy.) So, after we 'take a bath' we sit down at the table. We have with us two superiors of the Sisters of San José, Brazilians, who are visiting Irene and Edina.

Three other persons are sitting around us on the cement pavement next to the table. A woman who is very ill with meningitis and is very silent. A man, well along in years, whose wife deserted him a short time ago. And old Augusta, tall and very thin, all bones and skin, quite dark-skinned, with her white hair mussed, a blend of devout worshipper and prophetess, who has the gift of being able to speak with the liveliest phrases and images in the language of the people, in the midst of her spirited profusion of words. We ran into her in the street, she came with us, and here she is talking away.

I enjoy once again the *tucunaré*, that tasty fish from the Araguaia. It is fresh from the river and well-seasoned in the oven. Conversation about the various kinds of fish in this teeming Araguaia brings to our hands some piranha jaws that Sister Irene has collected and cleaned. Piranhas are those voracious carnivores that live in the Araguaia in fearsome schools. The teeth are perfect in shape and in whiteness, like the blade of a saw, razor sharp.

After dinner, as we sat talking, old Augusta wanted to leave, and the bishop said good-bye to her with this prophetic blessing: "May Jesus free you from all persecution. May your troubles leave you like the wind, away from the world, and may you be at peace."

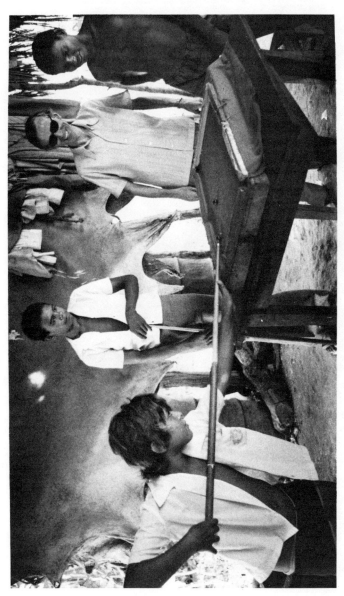

"I visit every house. I talk with everyone, absolutely everyone. And we talk about everybody and everything, realities, joys, problems."

"You ask me about my faith. . . .
I answer you with my life.
With the life of my world without justice and without voice."

9

Believer, Poet, Sinner

My Faith Leaves Me Naked

Night has wrapped the town in shadows. In the homes shine lamps of kerosene, of gasoline or oil and fat. The after-dinner talk went on and on and it became rather late. Ten o'clock around here is a very late hour, an hour to be asleep. Pedro and I must finish the dialogues because early tomorrow we separate. I have kept for this last night the most personal part of Pedro, the most intimate part, his faith, his poetry, and his sins.

On a small table, there by the trembling light of the candle, are the tape recorder and my notebook. Pedro and I are in the kitchen of Terezinha and Tadeu's house. In the room to one side—all the doors are open—already asleep in a hammock, lies the unbalanced boy who is working with Father Antônio. We talk quietly.

There is a good guide to knowing the bishop of São Félix as a believer. He was asked to write the autobiography of his faith, his creed, and he wrote it. *¡ Yo creo en la justicia y en la esperanza!* [I Believe in Justice and in Hope!]. Published in 1975, the book has been reprinted every year and has been translated into Italian, French, and English [Eng. trans: *I Believe in Justice and Hope* (Notre Dame: Fides Claretian, 1979)]. His book was upsetting and shocking, as was foreseen. In the prologue I warned him that some people would rend their garments and make accusations against him. Pedro's creed is too Christian and evangelical to be endured by certain "men of the church."

This particular moment and this warm night are a good opportunity for Pedro to review his faith and his creed.

"I have observed that Dom Sigaud based his dramatic accusations against you on the basis of citations from your 'creed.' Apart from the unpleasantness it must cause you to have it 'used' against your own faith, this is an important consequence of your book. Do you have echoes of other repercussions? What has this testimony of faith meant for people, in the church and in the town? Has it brought you anything but accusations and vexations?"

"Well, look, it seems to me that it has meant quite a bit because of a sad hereditary defect in this holy church of God. Because we esteem a bishop as we do, the fact that a bishop speaks with a certain simplicity and says what he thinks, and 'undresses a little' (as dear Father Llanos asked me to do in this book) is something new, different, that shakes and expands the hearts of many people. I know this from many letters that have come to me, saying thank God, finally someone who is a bishop has said what so many of us think but do not know how to or cannot express, above all with regard to intrachurch or intraecclesiastical problems. And also because the diary part has meant especially, for many people outside as well as inside Brazil, the discovery of a very shocking situation: the problem of farmers without land, of the homesteaders, of that tense day-to-day struggle of a church with the power of the big landowners and the forces of repression. And that desire that God has given us to become incarnate, to commit ourselves to this people, has also been (and this both shakes me and comforts me at the same time) a kind of testimony of the frontier.

"I already told you something of this before: we have meditated at times on the mission of churches like ours, obliged (and called upon) to be a little 'frontier' within the church because in the pastoral ministry, in liturgy, in mentality, and in organization—in everything—we find ourselves, whether or not we like it, a little on the frontier of what is permitted and not permitted, of what is done and not done, of what is experienced and not experienced. Likewise in the matter of 'ecumenical' (in quotes) dialogue, with those who say they are not in the church or think they don't even have faith, our church has been an open door, or at least a window, and we have felt that Christ made known to them his presence and that they looked at the church in a new way.

"I could give you an example if you like, perhaps a little personal and somewhat extreme. On the first visit I made to the chief political prisoners (I say 'chief' because they were a very significant nucleus), when I left—the lawyer told me later—they all asked for the Bible and they said that they had rethought several of their positions (most of them were Marxists, not Christians), and that they had sensed a different church and they had accepted in a spirit of dialogue the answers that I, spontaneously and without pretension, had offered at that time. And their hearts throbbed. Our hearts throbbed together with the same suffering and hope. Then other sectors of youth, including university students, also became interested. Something that ought to be daily and normal, what I said in my book, simply to give testimony to one's own faith and to say calmly what one thinks, is, unfortunately, exceptional. My book came to be providentially a sign, a testimony, a little like a prophecy, as you said. And once again I say that I do not wish to lapse into pedantry. Any Christian, any bishop could and ought to speak of his faith as he speaks of his sorrows and his joys."

"It's now three years since you wrote your 'credo,' in its two parts: 'the life that gives meaning to your creed' and 'the creed that gives meaning to your life.' Only a few days ago you wrote a thick appendix to 'the life that gives meaning to your creed,' telling what you have lived through in the past three years. I ask you: what articles or appendices would you now add to the creed that gives meaning to your life, or what articles would you delete from it?"

"Well, notice, when I was obliged to reread this creed now,

because of the translation, with a certain degree of calm (very relative calm, as you know), I found that almost everything I live through and feel, everything that concerns me and stimulates me and fills me with enthusiasm, I more or less said it or hinted at it then. Moreover, I am not a theologian, I am not a creator of new doctrines. I gather up, I know by intuition what others have said or have thought, and in short I express simply what I live, what makes me live. I would not now add anything. It seems to me that, rather, I would suppress articles from my creed. And not because I have ceased to believe in anything I said. I said in it that for me theology (I would now say faith), for me faith, like poetry for Juan Ramón Jiménez, is laying itself bare to me more and more. And as it opens to me, it becomes for me more friendly, more beloved, more intimate, more of me and more of God and more of both of us. It is like two or three basic tree trunks that support all the leaves and all the flowers and all the fruits of the earth and the heavens. God and people, people and God, and Jesus Christ in the middle, uniting God with people and people with God, and making them one people, which is the church. That church— which I am less and less able to define, because it seems to me more and more visible and invisible at the same time—it appears to me (I see it) more and more as a sacrament, with tangible and intangible elements; it seems to me more and more the world, and less and less the world. And it seems to me more and more recognized as such by the world, as it becomes more and more authentically what it should be, because it has less power, less worldly influence, even fewer words, to the extent that it adheres more and more to the great Word of the gospel. God, humanity, and Christ.

"And with this, I would even cut down a bit certain articles of my creed. I would shade them. For example, I spoke of the religious life: I am living it, I am grateful to it, I recognize it. It seems to me that because I am a religious I am what I am with respect to prayer and commitment to life, and because I am a religious *here*, in this Mato Grosso that has been for me the last great sacrament of my life.

He corrected himself energetically: "Or the next to the last! I hope that my death will be the last sacrament of my life.

"And about religious life, I believe that I would say now, thinking again of Brother Mateus, what he already felt by intuition, that with every passing day the religious life will become really 'poorer,' even scorned; it will have less and less status, it will every day embrace celibacy more and more, and as a form of poverty, as Arturo Paoli would say, even unrecognized at times within the church itself; the eunuchs of the kingdom of heaven. And the religious life will be truer to itself by reason of its incarnation, even sociopolitical, in the midst of the people. You understand perfectly what I mean when I say that. It's not a question of engaging or not engaging in politics; in a certain sense there is no way of not doing so, it's always done: depending on what you are, on how you live, you're already engaging in some kind of politics.

"I also think that in my expressions that refer more directly to Jesus Christ I would insist a little more on the aspects of the new figure of Jesus that several theologians have helped us to rediscover, to resee, to rethink, and to relive, as really being Jesus and the Christ, the Messiah and Jesus, and therefore being the Lord. I believe that there, in the synthesis that fulfills and simplifies things, I am understanding Jesus Christ better and better. I have relativized the Bible a good deal in its cultural aspects and at the same time it seems to me that I have also discovered quite a lot of what Jesus had and what he had to have on the cultural side, because being the 'incarnation' he couldn't be anything else. And it has helped me to understand the sociopolitical derivations of the gospel and of the life of Jesus, not formulated as such, and certainly not formulated into parties or into organizations, of course, or in terminology of more recent coinage, formulated into demands.

"With respect to Our Lady, as I already said, it is Our Lady of the Magnificat, more and more, and Our Lady of the Resurrection. When I refer to the Magnificat, I am referring to what she said about the poor. I'm not going to enter here into hermeneutical disquisitions, whether or not the Magnificat is hers, or to what extent it is or isn't. I am speaking of the Magnificat that she sang in her spirit even if she didn't sing it aloud. In any event, as far as I am concerned, she said what she said about the poor, and about the God of the poor, because she was really poor herself. And then Our Lady of the Resurrection: she really took on death, her death, the death of her people; she accepted (it is clear that she did) that her people was not the people that it dreamed of being, so that her son might be the resurrection and the life of all peoples—right?—and so that her own people might be the seed of the new people. It seems to me that that aspect is also extremely important. There probably are a thousand other shades of meaning.

"In politics I continue to think, more and more, that everyone, even a bishop, must take a specific stand in order to be faithful and honorable, and not to be left in the beautiful and comfortable and approved position of neutrality, and afterwards feel entitled to receive homage and benefits from both sides because one did not commit oneself. For the same reason, and without softening the trenchant political position I took before—and even intensifying it, when the aspect of incarnation is added—sorting things out in a *relative* framework, in the march of time, it seems to me more and more that the best road is socialism, a democratic socialism. As I said before, it isn't this or that political party, much less is it this or that country, although it can appear a little in and thanks to such and such a party in such and such a country. After all, diverse experiences are what make possible a 'more' perfect experience within the relativity of all things (the church included) in this time of our active hope. We are not yet in the era of eternity; we are in the era of relativity. So I believe that we ought to overcome the desire to link the faith too closely with any specific model of political programing. But of course we must (I repeat, must) always link the faith with a true sociopolitical commitment. This commitment will be translated into political parties; every Christian will see to it. And why not? As I can and must have opinions and attitudes in biology, in medicine, in literature, much more so must I have them in politics, which is much more vital."

"Why do you think that Dom Sigaud and the other ecclesiastical or lay 'Dom Sigauds' have misunderstood your creed so badly?"

"Simply because we use different hermeneutics. We all see according to the lens we are using. And we all use the lens that we think is correct for our own eyes. There is a kind of vicious circle here. I have nothing against him, I repeat once more; for me Dom

Sigaud is the expression of a certain political attitude and of a certain ecclesiastical attitude. I understand perfectly that he and others, if they do not live close to the people, and if they do not feel the tragedy of this people (I do not deny them good intentions, by no means, nor do I consider myself to be better, by no means), and if they think that the church is already eternal in essence and in its ways and manners, it is logical that they are frightened when I speak, for example, of celibacy tied or not tied to the priesthood; it is logical that they are frightened when I speak of socialism. And it's not only a question of theology. That difference of hermeneutics is carried over into the way of reading history, into the way of reading philosophy, not to speak of the way of reading daily life. It is a hermeneutical problem, which is the same problem we have when we read the Bible."

I here take note, objectively, of a very picturesque circumstance. When Pedro was confessing to me his faith in Jesus, rediscovered, rethought, and relived as Jesus and the Christ, as the Lord, the rooster in the neighboring yard crowed. And he crowed more than three times. And in response there was crowing from other distant roosters. Our whole dialogue this night is laced by the crowing of the roosters of Santa Terezinha. And to prove it, it shows up on the tapes.

If I'm Anything at All, I'm a Poet

"To jump to another theme: poetry. What did poetry mean to you formerly? Does it still mean anything now?"

Pedro listens to me and he laughs. He laughs with emotion.

"You are now plucking a 'frivolous' chord, as our novice masters would say—right?—but doubtless also human and holy. Poetry has meant and still means a lot to me. I think at times that if I am anything, it is that, a poet. Even as a religious and as a priest and as a bishop, I am a poet. Many things I know by intuition, I feel, I say, I do, because I am a poet. You know that for me poetry is the word of emotion, reality known by intuition and expressed in a word of emotion. So, well, you know me, you know how I feel, how I act, how I react. . . . I really think that poetry is a part of me. I said years ago that, in addition to giving up women and a career and who knows what else, I would also have to give up poetry. And then I recited a verse of Pemán."

He has become excited again. He laughs with emotion.

"I recited with a certain humor, with a certain deep-felt nostalgia, that verse that says: 'I gave up / the florid madness of that love / but I did not give up the pain / of that wound.' I have given up poetry as *the* mission of my life. I shall say to you, with complete simplicity, that I think I might have been a great poet. It seems to me that I had the talent and the desire to be one. Now, I have never given up poetry as expression, as an instrument. Clearly my poetry has been more clerical than the poetry of others, because after all I am a cleric. If I were married and had children I should sing to the wife and I should sing to the children. That's obvious."

He thinks. . . . He looks around him.

"I believe that poetry has meant a great deal in my life. That sensitivity, that intuition, an attitude of tenderness before nature, before all things, before people, before pain, before weakness, before pettiness, at times and under circumstances of exaltation also. I therefore believe that poetry has been for me much more than a hobby. It has been a psychological constituent, which has expressed me and through which I have expressed my faith and even my ministry."

"Do you feel there is a relation between poetry and prophecy, between being a poet and being a prophet?"

"It clearly exists. And I feel it. For me, every poet is a prophet (if you prefer, a lay prophet; I'm prepared to make distinctions that I don't like very much). Every poet listens to the heart of the people and translates it into a cry, an outcry. All poets give to their people, at the historic moment if they are more epic poets, or at the sentimental moment if they are more lyric poets, the word, the vision, the climate that makes the people vibrate, that gives it life. And the Bible itself has shown us that all prophets are poets. Moreover, I believe that depending on the sensitivity that one has, grace moves within one and acts within one. It is evident that in what is mathematical, grace will express itself mathematically, in experiences, in projects, in performances more certain, more exact, more precise. And in the person who is a poet, grace expresses itself in a poetic way."

A good part of the poetic work of Pedro Casaldáliga was collected in the book *Tierra nuestra, libertad* [Our Land, Liberty], published in Buenos Aires in 1973. Its first part, "Memory of Uriel," brings together some of the poems written up to 1964 for the Claretian poetry magazine, *Uriel*. The second part has all the Marian poems (1964–66) published by *Uriel* under the title *Llena de Dios y de los hombres* [Filled with God and with Men]. The third part is the integral text of *Clamor elemental* [Primordial Cry], a book published in 1971 with illustrations by Maximino Cerezo, a Claretian friend and working companion on our journal of testimony and faith, *Iris*. The "primordial cry" is the poems written by Pedro in the course of his first two years of living in Mato Grosso, poems that transmit all the vibrations of joy, of tenderness, of pain and anger, that he has felt faced with this nature and this people. The last part, which gives its title to the book, *Tierra nuestra, libertad,* has the twenty-six new poems that express the crudest and most agonizing problems; these are the most epic of Pedro's poems.

Recently he has written about some experiences deriving from humor and irony, without renouncing lyricism or testimony. As he says, "he whistles in verse" the serious things that can't be said in prose. Thus, the poems already quoted, "Psalm Half Hopeful and Half Melancholy of a Bishop Accused of Communism," "A Little Ballad of Death," and those verses that introduce this book, "These Raucous Roosters Answer You."

I have as a project to gather in a small book the "cursed poems" of Pedro Casaldáliga—those that most shocked Archbishop Sigaud and those that bear the most sorrow and the most denunciation, those of the most wounded love of Pedro in this struggle of impotence, of prophecy and of hope.[1] I am motivated by the certainty that, as Pedro himself says, if he is anything, he is a poet, and it is in his poetry that he best expresses the drama of his people, with its immense weight of faith and prophecy. His poems can transmit a testimony of humanity and the gospel, they can give voice to the cry of the peoples who clamor for justice, and the committed faith of a church that tries to offer them coherently (with prophecy and martyrdom) the good news of salvation.

"I Live in Examination of Conscience"

Antônio has lent his room to the two Josephite superiors and he has come to sleep also in this house of Terezinha and Tadeu. Now he hangs his hammock in the room next door. For hours Matos has been sleeping and snoring, reminding me again of the roars of his launch and the Araguaia.

This night hour of deep sleep, made into a vigil in the silence and the confidences of a friendship traversed by the faith that pacifies and disquiets, as the domestic crowing of the roosters pierces the night and its silence, joins with me in extending to Pedro this bold invitation:

"At the end of these dialogues I invite you to make aloud, sincerely and simply, an examination of conscience. As if this were the hour of truth."

Pedro looks at me submissively.

"I believe we would have to begin by singing the 'Gloria,' or something like that, wouldn't we? With a thanksgiving. I am thinking more and more that God will not judge us either for the good or the evil that we have done, but simply for whether we have been capable of accepting God's love and transmitting it to other people. And if we have been capable of loving God in other people, God will welcome us forever, and that will be the peace and the glory, right? Yes, I must begin by giving thanks to God for everything, because really everything has been the grace of God. And above all for that final great grace that has been now ten years in a row of suffering, of struggles, of persecutions, of anguish, of throbbing, of enthusiasms, of people, of church, of faith, of hope in this beloved Mato Grosso, this Amazonia, this church of Brazil, of Latin America."

He is silent, and I respect his silence, hoping that he will go on by himself.

"Now, I am living in a certain state of examination of conscience. I don't know. It so happens that I was thinking these days, I was thinking of writing it down in the diary and it slipped away from me, and now I don't remember very well, but I was thinking what were probably my main defects and my main good qualities."

"The defects. Let's have the defects first."

"If I look clearly at myself, I discover in myself something very familiar. The leopard doesn't change his spots. Impatience and touchiness. On the other hand, sensitivity, which often moves me to impatience but which also encourages intuition and tenderness. Besides that impatience, as a quality, I see a certain generosity, which is no merit of mine, it is in me, it is in my blood, a little of it is in my family and in circumstances. That would be the major reckoning that I would make of my life now.

"My examination here, in these years? I believe that God has no memory, fortunately. Then there is no need to concern oneself much about what is far in the past. Fortunately. God has already wiped it clean. Well, then, here in these years I have had my angers and my vanities. As I say in *La muerte que da sentido a mi credo* [The Death that Gives Meaning to My Creed], and as you and I were saying the other day, here in this church of São Félix I have seen myself in the pillory and on a pedestal. And that has provoked in me as much anger as vanity. I am vain, like everyone. Perhaps like you. As a poet, even more, our novice masters would say. It seems to me that it has not gone so far as to be pride. And as I have that wish, those yearnings, for silence and solitude, to be placed on a pedestal is for me often a sacrifice. I no longer can distinguish clearly between being on a pedestal and being in the pillory. Possibly it is all the same thing, which I hope may be only the cross, death-resurrection, for me, for the people, for this church, for the church as a whole. Those angers, moreover, have not been personal. Really I don't detest anyone. I don't hate anyone, I hold no rancor against anyone specifically, although I have cursed the big landowners and now I am beginning to curse the tourism that is arriving here. It seems to me that these may be angers distantly related to those of the prophets; even Jesus got angry, even at a great distance, right? He is the Lord. . . .

"At times I have been demanding. I used to accuse myself of impatience, and that impatience translates itself into excessive demands. At times I fear I have been demanding toward the pastoral team. And perhaps also at times toward the people themselves. And maybe that impatience may have wounded someone at some time. Occasionally, because of my impatience, I am rash, don't you agree? Even in not yet recognizing enough substance in popular religion. For example, some time ago, you noticed, I didn't like the artificial flowers that we found next to the sanctuary. I must say that now I feel quite at ease with the people's devotions and their singing. And this is not a tactic; I feel at ease, their things are my things. Once it could have been an attitude, now it is my life. Although I continue to be impatient and nervous, as you know, it seems to me that I have made myself more receptive. (I am searching my soul and singing my praises. Since you won't sing them, I sing them myself!)"

Pedro's sonorous guffaw is the voice of his slyness.

"Said with all simplicity, really. I confess to you also that at times I have felt fear for a kind of responsibility complex, with that sensitivity and vulnerability that I have always had. You know that when I was a child I was more grown-up than usual, even my elders told me that; I didn't have much of a childhood.

"I confess to you that I have also been concerned about whether I have done enough to save the church here, to the extent that I am a bishop. Through the training that we have had I ought to save it without any doubt, right? It has concerned me that I may have gone too far. Perhaps I have gone beyond that 'frontier,' as we say. Whether I shock others or not in my way of leading this church and even more so now that we have become something of a leading light. I wonder about this at times very seriously. But, as I told you in Luciara, when I again set my feet and my heart on the very harsh reality of these people, of these beloved souls, abandoned and oppressed to an unbelievable degree, it seems to me that I am not exaggerating, it seems to me that we are still falling short.

"Now, it may be that, really, for some I have been a source of scandal, a sign of contradiction and collision. I regret the grief I have caused, but it seems to me inevitable and, in the long run, healthy. I console myself a little at times by saying, to round off the famous saying that the bishop must be a sign of unity, that he must be as much a sign of contradiction as a sign of unity, if his sign comes from the Bible. It seems to me that the two things come from Christ himself, right? Nobody is going to say that Christ was only a sign of unity and not of contradiction, when he scattered everything, he scattered even his apostles.

"As for prayer, I've stopped praying automatically. For me, automatic prayers were always a torture. You know that I have never been capable of saying mechanically one after another the three parts of the rosary; I would get tongue-tied, my mouth would get cottony dry. But it seems to me that I'm open-minded about prayer. If we understand prayer as devotions, I say lauds every morning. I like to say them in company. We usually say them, we who are at home, in front of the sanctuary, with the reading of a meditation. At night I go on praying compline, even in Latin. I *do* skip the *tamquam leo rugiens,* but I soften and yield to the *in manus tuas commendo spiritum meum* because it's true and I feel it deeply. I continue paying visits to the Lord in the sanctuary. I appeal to Mary and I relate to her as a point of reference. And I continue to find pleasure in the celebration of the feasts of the saints, my friends. At times it bothers me that I can't feel more communitarian about team prayer, favoring pluralism which, as I said before, pulls together various options and services.

"As for public celebrations, there certainly are group celebrations, team celebrations, at meetings, at intense moments, but in principle and in practice, we try more and more to have the norm be celebrations by the people. Because it's a way of being the people, and otherwise we're a caste. In the celebration with the people, we take considerable freedom of spirit in the formulation, so that it is much more vital, but it is always paschal. We insist a great deal on the word, communicated, celebrated, dialogued; we converse, valuing highly the word but demythologizing the text, the book.

"If, as Arturo Paoli used to say to us during a retreat, to pray is to frequent the Lord Jesus, I believe that in all these sufferings, worries, afflictions, in this struggle and even in those contradictions, I persistently frequent the Lord Jesus. Appealing to him, living his passion, feeling his cross, crying out the force of his resurrection, seeking his word and his gestures, as keys of interpretation. Singing, too. One of my great prayers is song; singing with the people or alone, at various moments, even on long bus trips, I meditate and I sing; sometimes people think I'm cracked, though I don't sing at the top of my lungs, of course, but in a soft voice. I've become somewhat Teilhardian and I commune with nature and with the universal presence of God in everything and in everyone. In the presence of this most beautiful and most outraged nature I feel the unity and the presence of God. I used to believe that contemplation was not for me; now I am within myself more and more. On bus trips (I've traveled ten, twenty, thirty, forty, sixty hours in a row, two, three, four thousand miles), I meditate a lot."

I certify that this is Pedro, bishop of São Félix, in body and soul. That those are his sins. His "main defects and his main virtues." I certify that he is like this inside and out. This is known to all who live in his company. Could I, could any of us, name other defects of his, other virtues? I don't know if it would be possible. I believe that I could name other virtues, but, at any rate, it's unnecessary. This book is dialogue, nothing but dialogues. Open dialogues. Wide open . . .

Before returning to the night, and before leaving it, I *am* going to allow myself to ratify that this Pedro who said to me "I believe that if I am anything, I am a poet," and to whom I say "if you are anything, you are a poet of prayer," in fact does frequent the Lord Jesus. I certify it with this prayer-poem that Pedro wrote at one of the harshest and most critical moments of his life:

> LORD JESUS!
>   *An Enquiry into Subversion*
> You are
> my strength and my failure
> my heritage and my poverty.
> You my justice,
> Jesus.
>
> My war
> and my peace.
> My free freedom!
>
> My death and my life,
> you.
> Word of my cries,
> silence of my waiting,
> witness of my dreams,
> Cross of my cross!

Cause of my bitterness,
forgiveness of my egotism,
crime of my trial,
judge of my poor tears,
reason of my hope,
you!

You are
my promised land . . .

The Easter of my Easter,
our glory
forever,
Lord Jesus!

Those roosters that crow tonight in Santa Terezinha cannot be simply the roosters of the sin of Saint Peter. They must be (at least in addition) the roosters of the first hour of the Sabbath, when Peter was led by the Spirit toward the signs of the Resurrection. And (at least in addition) they could be the roosters of the martyred afternoon of that Pedro who was led, by the enemy and the spirit, to where he would not have wanted to go, but he consented to be led because of the promise of Jesus the Christ, the Messiah, the Lord.

"May Jesus free you from all persecution.
May your troubles leave you like the wind, away from the world,
and may you be at peace."

Farewell

Pedro went off this morning, with Matos, in the launch. They will go up the Araguaia to São Félix. With them went Lucio, a young homesteader from Santa Terezinha who is going to be examined in the hospital. He had great circles under his eyes and a pale face. He spat frequently. They wonder if he may have turberculosis complicated by some kind of leprosy.

Pedro's farewell has filled me with strength and nostalgia. Our last words, on the way to the dock, were few and interrupted by greetings to the people whose paths we crossed, with whom we talked in the doorways or in the square, next to the jail. At the back of the square is the river. On the bank Pedro said: "For my friends over there, you are my letter and my message. Give them all that we have and are, and what we are hoping for." We hugged each other tightly and he stepped onto the launch. Lucio wrapped himself in a red shawl. At Pedro's feet I saw an enormous fresh pineapple and a heap of lemons. Matos started the motor and Pedro, standing with his back to the wind, gave me the victory signal with his hands held high until they were lost in the immense Araguaia. Now it is noon. Antônio and I seek refuge from the sun that is burning the bare red soil of the small airport. We are waiting for the twin-engine plane that, on a regular flight, will take me to Brasilia.

Two small planes land in succession. Tadeu appears, who left a

173

week ago from Goiãnia. The bus couldn't come all the way because the floods made some highways impassable. After a three-day wait in São Félix he got a seat on a *teco* (air taxi) that was coming back. The price of a return trip was bearable.

After a wait shorter than that at any big airport, our twin-engined plane reached its relative height over the *roças* (cultivated land), the countryside and the jungle, the river and the whole immense backwoods.

On this flight I sat next to the owners of the Floating Hotel of the Araguaia, that enemy ship kept at bay off the lake of the Tapirapé Indians—a gentleman, tall and so stout that he found it difficult to accommodate his perimeter in the small plane seat, and his wife, who hides the age in her face with colors robbed from the sun and from the make-up box. They are German. They resolutely speak a Portuguese harshened by a German accent. With them is a pretty German girl, a stewardess, and a Brazilian with his wife (whose nationality I do not know because she doesn't say a word). They all have very sunburnt faces and arms, and they have with them objects of native handicraft: bows, arrows, handbags, jars. The owners of the hotel talk steadily for the benefit of their tourist friends, pointing and showing them, in their way, the countryside, the farms, the Araguaia, Santa Tere-zinha, the Tapirapé village, Luciara. . . . And so I leave behind, on this flight, the places that I passed on the river, listening to and imagining this "other" way of seeing, living, and telling about the world of the Mato Grosso. I feel sharply the contrast and I am strongly assailed by the memory of Pedro, his friends, his people, the homesteaders, the peons, the Indians, the naked children with swollen bellies, their eyes, their faces, their dramas. . . .

"This whole wooded territory was sold to some Americans for the orange trees. They just saw it from the plane and they bought it as if it were an orange grove." The tourists greet with laughter this information from the owner of the hotel, while the motors spread their roar through the green forests that I look out at.

We stop at Santa Isabel on Bananal Island. And I have São Félix a boat-length away, opposite me, on the other side of the Araguaia. As we take off, I can make out the streets of the town, I look at their houses going by, and I give a last glance to the house with the porches and the hammocks, and to the new cathedral church (Pedro, Irene, Pedrito, Cecilia, Vera . . .).

We fly low enough for me to see clearly the woods violated by the landowners. There is already smoke from the giant fires that smother so much life to make way for the cattle of the lord-possessors of the lands. "The ox is worth more here than the native." I see the great estates, I see their fences, the barbed wire of this unjust war. I hold in my hands Pedro's poem "Our Land, Liberty," and I reread:

> Conceited prostitutes
> of the common mother,
> their ill-born!
> Curséd be
> your fences,
> the ones that surround you
> from within,
> fat,
> alone,
> like fattened pigs;
> with your barbed wire and your titles
> shutting
> out of your love
> your brothers and sisters!
>   (Out of their rights,
>   their children
>   and their tears
>   and their dead,
>   their arms and their rice!)
> Shutting yourselves
> out from your brothers and sisters,
> and from God!
>
> Curséd be
> all fences!
> Curséd be all
> private property
> that deprives us
> of life and love!
> Curséd be all laws
> twisted by a few hands
> to protect fences and oxen

and to make the earth a slave
and our brothers and sisters slaves!

Our earth is everybody's earth!
Human earth, free earth, brothers and sisters!

Roaring, the plane flies through a gigantic whirl of clouds. The forest is left behind and the Araguaia is lost on the right. We reach the green plains with their hills, new rivers and wide red roads. We leave Mato Grosso and head toward Brasilia. "Sky-and-garden city / in other times. / Brasilia today is scarcely / an antechamber, / structures, / an audience without ears, / March without spring. . . ." I take refuge in Pedro's poems. *Our Land, Liberty.* This copy he sent to me three years ago, inscribed in his flourishing hand. Now the inscription means much more to me:

Teófilo, my brother: The liberty of the children of God is our earth; the soil where we must sow life; the humus of the new world. The earth is the space of our liberty! From this Brazilian earth of mine, from my struggle for the land of the landless, from my exodus with the people, from my hope, I send you an embrace of total communion in Christ. *Pedro.*

I reread some poems and I am revived. . . . The dialogue continues to be open. And Pedro's words, the rise and fall of his voice, his laughter, the roosters in the night, the songs of the people, the Araguaia and its beaches, the grief of the people, so many, many faces, some with names, some without, so many children, so much sickness, the huge moon, the tree-covered hills, the herons, the *tucunaré*, the cows, the dogs of the Tapirapé village, all the Indians, the swift fishes in the reddened sunset lake, the Little Sisters, all the young people, Wampú, the hope, the fear, death lurking. Everything revives in me, everybody lives in me. I no longer hear the voices of the owners of the hotel, the shout of the motors—barely a distant murmur. "And the soul of the forest / now / is in my hands. / The people is in my weeping, like an importunate fetus / to whom is denied the sun, / liberty, / the human voice, / life. . . ."

"The liberty of the children of God is our earth, the soil where we must sow life, the humus of the new world. The earth is the space of our liberty! From this Brazilian earth of mine, from my struggle for the land of the landless, from my exodus with the people from my people I send you an embrace of total communion in Christ."

"For me, the church is not even a society. The church is the ferment of the new society. The church is light, it is salt, it is the seed in humanity."

Postscript: Between Regression and Hope

This dialogue, held with Pedro in August 1980, is a special updating of the situation for my English-language readers. In Brazil 1980 was the year of a terrible economic crisis. It was also the year of a political "opening-up," after fifteen years of iron-fisted military dictatorship. With the opening-up came the bombs, bombs to terrify and kill so that openness would not end up in democracy.

1980 was also the year of the pope's trip to Brazil. "João de Deus," John of God, went through thirteen Brazilian cities, speaking to the state and the church, the poor and the rich. But he clearly leaned toward the church and the poor. In the history of Brazil it was the greatest religious and popular event that people could remember. Twenty million Brazilians poured into the streets to see the "White Symbol" coming on God's behalf to give hope to the poor, suffering people, to defend their lives and violated rights, and to demand justice for them. Practically all Brazilians, more than 100 million of them, let themselves be carried away by this alluring figure and his words, which were reported on radio and TV as well as in the press.

In Latin America 1980 was the year of a struggle to the death, as the people of Central America sought to liberate themselves from military dictatorships. "A free country or death!" cried Nicaragua. Many Nicaraguans died in the struggle, but the people of Nicaragua were freed from the tyranny of the Somozas. The Sandinista Front has joined the people in trying to rebuild Nicaragua while serious anti-Marxist worries plague the United States, the anticommunist countries of Latin America, and the church of CELAM and the Vatican.

It was a year of death and murder, without truce or end, in El Salvador and Guatemala. It was a year of martyrdom for the people and the church. It was the year that saw the assassination of that great martyr for the poor, Oscar Arnulfo Romero, the hope of the people in San Salvador. "The blood of a continent will not do/ to wash us of this death" (Pedro Tierra).

It was also a year of regression to anticommunism. The cruel Nazi coup of García Meza in Bolivia choked off the democratic process of free elections, suffocating it in bestiality and bloodshed. And the pact reached by the nations of the southern cone bore witness to their stale anticommunism and their opposition to the U.S. policy of defending human rights. A despondent Carter, caught between the hostage crisis with Iran, the Russian invasion of Afghanistan, and his own re-election campaign, grew silent about human rights, which continue to be brutally violated.

In short, Brazil and all Latin America is caught between peaceful or violent openings to liberation and regression, between hope and regression. The church in Latin America is suffering through the same existential contradiction. "This is the topic I will bring up to Pedro for discussion," I mused, as I flew with Isidro from Brasilia toward the Araguaia River.

Another Dialogue in Mato Grosso

"Pedro is in Luciara," says Aunt Irene in São Félix. "The festivities for the patron saints of Luciara are taking place." So we head for Luciara—Isidro, myself, and Matos, our friend who knows the Araguaia like the palm of his hand. He unveils for us its hidden, fugitive life, pursuing it by boat as we hunt alligators through the water. Matos takes us to the bare beaches of the ever youthful river, uncovering nests of baby birds in the sand as their mothers chirp admonishingly in the air above. He traces the tracks of the tortoise back to its nest of eggs, points out birds and fishes to us, and chats with the Indians who are rowing their way to Luciara. Now low in water and teeming with life, the Araguaia will swell with the rains until it almost inundates these peoples and their lands.

We catch sight of Luciara in the distance. There on the shore the awnings of its shops are already stretching out to greet the wind and the first rays of the sun.

The headquarters of the pastoral team in Luciara is the same, but the members of the team are not. Clelio, Teresa, and Aninha are not there. Silvia and Sergio arrived a few months ago. Silvia is a woman of the plains, who has come to work with the Paresí Indians. She is part of *Operación Ancheta*, which is made up of lay volunteers who serve the Indians. From the Indians she learned the art of plaiting and weaving fiber threads. She made a paten and a chalice for Pedro which I now carry with me, a momento doubly personal. Sergio is a young Italian. With his curly hair and beard he seems to have escaped from a painting by Michelangelo. Silvia and Sergio are just coming in with some Carajá Indians. The team headquarters is filled with people because the team had taken in an old woman whose children have come for the festivities in Luciara. Pedro is not there. "He's gone to the church for a meeting that began at 7:00 A.M." It is now 9:00 o'clock. We head for the church through the dusty, sunburnt streets. But the church is locked and their is no sign of Pedro. The sun is unbearable, so we decide to wait for him back at the house.

Sergio comes out of the house with his fishing pole. "To the Araguaia, to get something to eat." Every single morning and evening Sergio brings back "our daily fish" from the Araguaia, that inexhaustible mother of delicious species. That particular day he brought back such noble specimens as piranha and corvina, each of the latter sporting a stone in its head like a mother-of-pearl. Silvia cooked them for us in the fire. Such tasty fish, no matter how cooked, cannot be found in any restaurant in the world.

Pedro, we learned, spends every morning visiting families in their homes and lunches with a different family every day. He returns later, his thin body shaded a bit by a blue sun visor on his cap. We surrender to the hard hugs through which our bones recognize each other, and then to endless talk. It is a never-ending banquet with Pedro, Free Speech incarnate.

We talk and talk when we can—mornings, evenings, nights—between the precious hours when he meets his people. (I went with him to such meetings at all hours in his church: 7:00 A.M.; 2:00 P.M.; 7:00 P.M.; catechetics lessons and liturgical celebrations where the word of God and the sacraments fused with the lives and problems and struggles of his people.) We talked on the porch, near the well, in the shade of a mango tree that gently filtered the light of the sun through to us. Sometimes, talking endlessly, we glimpsed the red-hot sun slip away from us. The shadows overtook us and the moon became our night-light. It was still Mato Grosso, the scenario of all our dialogues.

"Perhaps the key question is regression or progress," I said to Pedro. "Umm," says Pedro, tensing into one his gaze and thought and speech. "Between regression and the affirmation of hope." He ponders. I parcel out the subject a bit to get things going. "Consider it in terms of society and the church. Then, more generally, in terms of Brazil and Latin America. And what are your major concerns right now? And do you have any new poems to offer?" And so we were off and running.

Social and Ecclesiastical Regression

"There is no such thing as the *gift* of regression," said Pedro firmly. "Regression certainly is a fact, but it is not exactly a gift of the Spirit. Rather, it is an antidote used against the Spirit."

"What instances of regression would you point to in our society?"

"These openings-up are fallacies. They are instances of sheer opportunism on the part of multinational imperialism, which needs something to maintain itself. Latin America will end up as one big Wild West ranch, but with no redskins to be seen and all the horses turned into livestock. There we glimpse the new phases of the Trilateral Commission's machinations. Take the 'Yellow Peril' that now threatens Brazil. Under the pretense of progress and development the Brazilian government has entered an agreement with the Japanese government. Sixty million hectares of land have been set aside for exploitation and export by the Japanese. And the Brazilian government will help them by giving tax exemptions and providing needed infrastructures. In a racist, downright fascist gesture, it has been decided that one-third of the personnel will be Japanese (the bosses), another one-third will be Brazilians who are addicted to European ways and efficiency, and the final one-third will be poor laborers from Goiás and Minas Gerais. The poor will serve as menial manual laborers, as the peons of the enterprise. It is the old policy of immigration and farm labor to keep Brazil locked in its foreign debt. And political regression is obvious in the southern cone of South America, particularly with the new coup in Bolivia and the new pacts."

"And what about the ecclesial, or should I say ecclesiastical, arena?"

"In worldwide terms," replies Pedro, "there are questions being raised about the current pope. Where exactly does he stand between loyalty to his Catholic identity and obsessive concern with that particular identity?" Pedro ponders a bit before proceeding. "Isn't this the right moment to affirm one's Christian identity and complete fidelity to the faith? Isn't this the right moment to bear forceful witness to poverty, even on one's trips? Is the pope being more Polish than Catholic?"

When John Paul II was visiting Brazil, Pedro and I met in Fortaleza. I was covering the pope's trip for Madrid's *Vida Nueva*. Pedro was there for John Paul II's meeting with the Brazilian bishops on July 10. The pope was to inaugurate the National Eucharistic Congress. At that meeting between Pedro and myself, we concentrated on the positive aspects of the pope's visit: his fine way of getting along with the people and the church of Brazil. He encouraged them in their "noble struggle for justice," while insisting that they consistently avoid violence and class struggle.

Pedro had positive things to say about the papal trip then: "I think that John Paul II really supported his fellow bishops in Brazil and their national episcopal conference. I think this is the most positive thing he did for the people and the church in Brazil. By warmly praising the national episcopal conference of Brazil, he implicitly confirmed its line of action and its documents. He even made a point of saying that he was impressed by the simplicity of the Brazilian episcopate and its involvement with the common people. Secondly, I think that John Paul II's gestures were very worthwhile, more worthwhile than anything he said. His deeds expressed simplicity and closeness to the people. My impression is that the pope discovered much about the people on his trip to Brazil. Perhaps he discovered more here than he could on any other continent: i.e., structured, institutionalized, wretched poverty. Despite all the reservations one might legitimately have about such trips, I would say that the pope, the head of the Catholic church, was able to breathe some good 'catholic' air here. It should stand him in good stead in the Vatican, where such air is needed."

Verse Prophecies for the Pope

Now, back in Mato Grosso some time later, Pedro steps back a bit and becomes more critical. "To touch and move people does not always mean to convince them." Pedro has many questions about the papal trip. "Of course there can be no doubt whatsoever about his apostolic good will. Yet I am forced to reject the trappings of triumphalism and the unjustified expenses. Some things could be done so much more simply. And there was a certain amount of 'Catholic' manipulation of the people and the communications media. And the same goes for the authorities. They are delighted to call themselves Catholics in the pope's presence, yet at the same time they are persecuting and torturing the people and members of the church. They welcome the pope but turn their backs on justice."

Pedro grabs me by the arm and looks straight into my eyes: "These trips, like all noisy affairs, easily turn into useless waste. Doesn't the figure of the pope turn into needless waste in the eyes of the world when that happens to the figure of John Paul II?"

Pedro withdraws his grip and adds: "Besides, the pope did not come alone. He was accompanied by such people as Archbishop Marcinkus from the United States, who is regarded as unacceptable here."

Pedro continues to be a poet, achieving his own personal synthesis of prophecy and poetry. "One can say in verses what one cannot say in prose." He wrote a poem for John Paul II while he was travelling for two whole days by bus from São Félix to Fortaleza in order to attend the Brazilian bishops' meeting with the pope. John Paul II delivered a very appreciative address to the Brazilian bishops, praising them for their poverty and their commitment to their people. When the floor was opened to questions and the discussion of problems, Pedro got to the microphone eventually. He told the pope he did not have a question or a problem to pose. He simply wanted to read a poem to him. And he read the following verses:

JOHN PAUL, SIMPLY PEDRO

John Paul,
Simply Pedro.

Gather us together around the rejected stone,
Stones laid bare to the sun.
Confirm your brothers in the freedom of the Wind,
Fisherman.
Confirm our faith with your love.

Give us the audience of prophecy
And the encyclical with a pastor's sting.
The tribunal of the poor
Judges our mission.
The Good News,
Today as always,
Is news of liberation.
The Spirit has descended on the multitude.
The Curia is in Bethlehem
And on Calvary stands
The Major Basilica.

> It's time to shout with our whole lives
> That the Lord is alive.
> It's time to face the new *imperium*
> With the ancient purple of the Passion.
> It's time to love unto death itself,
> To give the greatest proof.
> It's time to fulfill the Testament,
> Forging communion in the ecumene.
>
> John Paul,
> Simply Pedro.

Amid the applause of the assembled bishops Pedro handed his poem to John Paul II, saying: "From one brother to another, from one poet to another." The pope shook hands warmly and uttered a sincere "Thank you" in Portuguese.

Pedro had also written a poem in memory of the late Pope John Paul I. It was brief, as his pontificate had been:

JOHN PAUL I

> He may or may not have been a sailor,
> Fit for the high seas and their risks.
> But he was a fisherman,
> Nets open in a smile,
> And he gathered us all in.
>
> He died in august, canonical solitude,
> Far removed from the open belly
> That hallowed Simon Peter's nakedness.

From Paul VI to John Paul II: The Vatican and CELAM Turn Inward

"We have seen the creation of what might be called a doctrine of Ecclesiastical Security, with its own processes, norms, and controls. Opus Dei clearly came to the forefront and gained special attention from the pope, who also showed greater tolerance for

Lefebvre. In Paul VI this regression was little more than a personal anxiety for fidelity when his strength failed him. A tense, creative life gave way to senility. The familiar surroundings of the Roman Curia became the decision-making center in the final days of an old man who had confronted things that no one would confront."

Our dialogue had come around to this debated epoch, which later history will see and judge more clearly than we can now. Pedro continued his line of thought: "After Paul VI and the enigmatic surprise of John Paul I, the institution, the various structures of conservation, and certain comfortable episcopates were looking for a spare part that had great reserves of sympathy and vitality as well as strong powers of communication. Their aim was to make regression total, to universalize the restoration of order in the framework of some New Christendom or some New Catholicism."

Pedro keenly feels the need we have to apply prophecy within the church in the quest for evangelical freedom and purity. Weighing his words carefully, he said: "The Vatican, as it has crystallized over the course of history right up to the present day, is the greatest enemy of the mission that Christ entrusted to Peter. After all, it is an internal enemy. It is a structure hostile to the witness, service, and evangelical form that Christ obviously wanted for his church. I was deeply impressed one day by the bold sincerity of Paul VI, when he said that he felt himself to be the greatest obstacle to ecumenism."

Pedro turned to contemplate a mango tree, which provides us with fruit and shade. "It is the maternal fecundity, the perduring fecundity of the Third World. It is our daily bread and fruit. In every poor person's yard there is a welcome spread of mango trees, like the broad lap of a mother. I haven't yet told this tree all that I have to say to it. I've written one poem about it, but I owe it another."

Pedro returns to our conversation, as if to a hard job. "The regression of the church in Latin America has taken concrete shape in CELAM, which is now obsessively trying to recover what it could not force through at Puebla." His hopes for the Puebla Conference, too, had found expression in a poem, as had his disappointment afterwards:

Before Puebla

Puebla of the angels:
Be Puebla of human beings;
Be Puebla of the martyrs;
Be Puebla of the poor;
Be Puebla of this people
in our America.

When the Conference was over, Puebla became a lamentation in verse:

After Puebla

Puebla, hope dampened
For this America stretched
Between Cross and Sword.

Ah, CELAM, how you mistrust us,
Trimming wind and sails
When the sea calls for action!

Alas, Puebla that has not yet been!
Puebla that we will have to fashion
From united ranks of the People.

"This CELAM," says Pedro, "creates courses run by remote control that hedge and vacillate. It puts obstacles in the way of encounters, movements, and meetings. In large measure it denies the basic evangelical rights of the local churches. It pours out journals and texts that are markedly restrictive and one-sided, that are filled with suspicion rather than encouragement. In the things promoted and published by CELAM you do not find the gift of courage and wisdom; instead you find the false gift of fearful suspicion. Whether it be witting or unwitting, what kingdom and what empire does it serve? The multinational empire can hardly find much in CELAM to object to. CELAM promotes ambiguous campaigns like its present one in Nicaragua.

Under the pretense of the sudden realization that ecclesial aid was needed, it enters the picture to indoctrinate and check up on things. As if to suggest that the Nicaraguan church was just coming to be after the Sandinista victory! As if there had been no need for assistance before, during Somoza's reign! So the danger has only arisen with the victory of the Sandinistas? So there were no abuses, no needs, no dangers before, with Somoza? For the people of Nicaragua light and liberty have dawned with the Sandinista victory. For CELAM that victory marks the beginning of chaos and disaster.

"What is more painful in evangelical terms is the fact that on the institutional level we seem to be capable of action only when it is a matter of being on the alert 'against' something. The positive gift of faith, it would seem, is to be turned into a negative mechanism of mere opposition. Is the church of Christ supposed to provide nothing but a service of negation and restriction when it comes to the struggles of humanity! There's not much fidelity in that sort of fidelity! It hardly seems to express loyalty to the man who risked being faithful unto death, and a scandalous death at that!"

Gains for the Church in Latin America

Pedro is not a pessimistic, belly-aching critic by nature. If he has a superabundance of anything it is a superabundance of hope. In him prophecy is a creative force. Criticism is only one dimension of his prophetic creativity. So in our conversations Pedro expatiated much more often on the advances and fresh gains being made by the church in Latin America.

"Over against the signs of regression, thank God, we find that the Latin American church committed to the people has achieved a calm, mature fidelity. It consists in remaining rebelliously but stubbornly loyal to the institutional church, to tradition as fleshed out and lived in the Latin American and Amerindian way, and to the truly catholic novelty of the Spirit, which need not be everywhere European or Latin.

"The local churches are growing increasingly aware that they form the basis of the church with their own accents, freedoms, and experiences.

"The base-level écclesial communities (CEBs) are continuing on their own course forthrightly and fearlessly. They humorously look on at a distance as some top leaders and canonical theorists express grave concern.

"Theologians have not been able to offer a completely satisfactory formulation for the new ministries in evidence. Yet these ministries are in fact being carried out with full official recognition and in complete communion with church pastors.

"And then we have the people and their achievements. The latter come in large measure from the womb of the CEBs and are helped along by pastors and Latin America's theologians. The sound good sense of our theologians, which can be measured in terms of realism, is particularly helpful. (By the way and thank God, I must admit that in 1980 the good and great theologians of Europe have accorded due recognition to the fine theologians of the Third World. To me this has been one of the nicest gestures of the church in the First World to the church of the Third World. I still believe that where you find ideas, you find life—both in ecclesial society and human society in general. Or perhaps I should say that life continues there, since life is the wellspring and seedbed of ideas. Well, enough of these Teresa-like tangents.) I was talking about the people and their achievements. The people of God are overcoming the dichotomy which we say in theory that we want to overcome: the dichotomy that denies and blocks incarnation. (I know that incarnation isn't everything, but it is the start of everything.) Overcoming this dichotomy, the people are celebrating the faith, creating labor unions, enlisting in the opposition forces, and creating ties and organisms for workers of every sort at the national and continental level.

"I cannot help but recall and admire the valiant nun who spoke out to the pope when he visited the United States. With heroic firmness and solid grounding she addressed him about the rights of women in the church, which are scandalously trodden under foot. I would only say that here in Latin America, in our base-level church communities, it is often some woman who is the inspirational leader in our public prayers and celebrations. There is no repression or protest of this fact based on class or *machismo*.

"Then there is the courage of pastoral agents and labor leaders, facing up to hired gunmen, the police, and the bigshots of this world even if it means death—martyrdom. When the worker named Rossi greeted John Paul II in São Paulo's Murumbí Stadium, he paid tribute to the memory of two murdered companions: Santo Díaz, pastoral agent and labor leader; and Raimundo "Gringo," pastoral agent and farm-workers' organizer."

Pedro has come to a topic that he feels deeply about, and which is an intrinsic part of his own life: martyrdom.

"Here in the Latin American church martyrdom has become one potential vocation in the ordinary course of things. In this respect, too, the Latin American church bears a strong resemblance to the virgin church of the first centuries. But along with the real martyrdom of flesh and blood we now experience, we must also suffer through another kind of martyrdom. For we find that large segments of the church in Latin America and around the world ignore, disregard, and remain silent about a reality of such Christian magnitude as that of martyrdom. It is an inexplicable and unpardonable oversight, a fearfulness that cannot be justified in Christian terms. Puebla's silence about these martyrs! John Paul II's silence about these martyrs when he visited Brazil! Kept at a distance by curia officials and colleagues, how Romero must have suffered through his agony! It is incomprehensible that the church of the crucified Lord is acting afraid of blood. Has it forgotten that it was ransomed at the cost of bloodshed?"

Pedro paid homage to his admired colleague, Archbishop Romero, in a lengthy poem that deserves to be quoted in full:

ST. ROMERO OF AMERICA, PASTOR AND MARTYR

The angel of the Lord declared in the evening . . .

The heart of El Salvador took note
Of the 24th, of March and of agony.

You were offering up the Bread,
                              the living Body,
The pulverized Body of your People,

Their Blood, spilt and victorious—
The peasant blood of your people massacred
That is to tinge the longed-for dawn
In wines of joy.

The angel of the Lord declared in the evening,
And the Word became death, once more, in your death.
As it does each day in the naked flesh of your people.

And it became new life
In our old church!

Once again we have Witness,
St. Romero of America, our pastor and martyr!
Romero of peace, a peace almost impossible
In this land at war.
Romero in purple flower,
The flower of our continent's untarnished hope.
Romero of our Latin American Easter.

Poor pastor now in glory,
Murdered by money,
            by the dollar,
                     by foreign currency,
Like Jesus, by order of the empire.
Poor pastor now in glory,
               abandoned
By your confreres of the crozier and the Communion table.

(The curias could not understand you:
No well-fixed synagogue can understand Christ.)

Your "poor flock" did attend you,
                       faithful in their despair,
Feeding your prophetic mission
                  even as they were fed.
The people made you a saint.
The hour of your people hallowed you as *kairos*.
The poor ones taught you to read the gospel message.

Like a brother
                  smitten
                           by so much sibling death,
You learned to weep alone, in the Garden.
You learned to be afraid,
like a warrior in battle.
But you also learned to give to your word,
The sound of freedom's bell.

And you knew how to drink your twofold chalice
    of the altar and the people
With a single hand, consecrated to service.

Latin America has already set you
    with all the glory of Bernini
In the halo-foam of its seas,
In the age-old altarpiece of the Andes,
In the wrathful canopy of all its forests,
In the song of all its pathways,
In the new Calvary of all it prisons,
                          all its trenches,
                          all its altars,
And the secure altar of its children's sleepless heart!

St. Romero of America, our pastor and martyr,
No one will silence your final Homily!

"Regrettably," sighs Pedro, "some manage to recognize the ecclesiastical martyrs but forget about the common people who are
martyrs in El Salvador, Guatemala, Bolivia, Nicaragua. These are
not drops of blood, but collective rivers of blood."

Then he goes on to stress "the openness to poverty displayed by
pastoral agents, bishops, priests, nuns, and lay people in particular. This is powerful witness within the church, and a powerful
protest against the idolatrous world of consumptionism.
. . . And the church of the mimeograph machine has continued
to expand in a much more organic way. Now publications spread
through whole nations and even the whole continent, reporting
experiences, essays, memoranda, songs."

Concluding Thoughts

It was getting late. It was time to sum up because I would soon have to leave. I asked Pedro to say something about Brazil, São Félix, and his own personal concerns and feelings.

"In Brazil we have seen progress: the strengthened role of the Brazilian National Episcopal Conference; the consolidation of CIMI and its recognition by activist anthropological and indigenist forces; and the spread of the CPT. The self-assertiveness of laborers and the Indians has been encouraged. The church of the Brazilian people has gained much credibility in Brazil and the whole world, even in the eyes of various political fronts. The forward march of the people, encouraged by the Latin American church, seems irreversible. We may get another Pinochet or another coup in Bolivia, but the march of the people will not be stopped.

"In the São Félix prelature the pastoral team, which once felt obliged to step in and play a necessary role, now wishes to imitate John the Baptist. We want to decrease in importance so that the people-in-Christ may increase in importance. We are handing over power to the people. The supreme decision-making body of this prelature is the assembly of the people, which is made up of representatives from all the local communities.

"All the various 'temporal' organizations—unions, parties, welfare associations, school associations, etc.—are establishing their independence. But note how our use of the word 'temporal' still bears traces of our tendency to set up a dichotomy between two realms or worlds. In any case our prelature is producing its own pastoral tools, pamphlets, and catechetical materials. The Vozes publishing house puts out some of these materials.

"One serious question that still preoccupies me personally is the 'how' of the priestly ministry. I believe in a twofold priesthood: that of celibates and that of married people. I believe, and I insist, that every Christian community has a right to its own minister for the celebration of the Eucharist. I am deeply worried about the regression of our seminaries. It is not the way. Seminarians must be asked to involve themselves in prayer, study, work, poverty, sharing life with the people, and pastoral practice (not just on weekends). There must be a realistic, day-to-day chance for them to determine their own vocations. We must move beyond the present hastiness to ordain people in order to make sure we get them. Priestly ordination must follow upon a certain level of attained maturity. We don't need flat tires, we need new tires filled with the breath of the Spirit."

I listened to Pedro as he recited a poem which expressed his own personal experience of celibacy:

A CELIBATE'S SONG

By night a virgin maid,
By day a boy,
Savage but beautiful,
I go on creating my peace.

I live out my loneliness,
Begetting a people all the while.
And my heart grows ever newer
As it grows old.

Wedding myself to hope,
I have espoused all love.
My inheritance is complete
In the Cross of my Lord.

Travelling alone, I return
Bearing my brood.
And my homeland is
The countenance of God.

With no comments or questions, I sit listening to Pedro: "I think I have learned how to listen, thought I'm still impulsive. I have learned to see things in relative terms, though I'm still sensitive. The flute of tenderness is still in my hands and lips, and the first breath of wind . . ."

Mary continues to be an important personage in Pedro's life.

She inspires him in his concern for the mission of the church and its ongoing purification. In one poem he associated her with Pentecost:

MARY OF PENTECOST

Mary of Pentecost,
When the church was still poor and free
As the wind of the Spirit.

Mary of Pentecost,
When the fire of the Spirit
Was the church's law.

Mary of Pentecost,
When the Twelve had nought to show
But the power of their witness.

Mary of Pentecost,
When the church was all mouth,
Mouth of the Risen One.

All these remarks I took down as I spoke with Pedro about regression on the one hand and the affirmation of hope on the other. In my memory I cherish many other conversations I had in Luciara with Pedro, Isidro, and Manuel. The sun and moon of the backlands were our witnesses.

On Thursday, August 28, 1980, I got up promptly at 4:00 A.M.; I called Isidro, who was sleeping under a net alongside me. There were about twelve such nets in the headquarters, with a person sleeping under each one. I found Manuel and woke him up too. Sergio, our fisherman, had crawled out of his net and was making coffee for us. The bus for São Félix would depart at 5:00 A.M. It was time to give a final hug to Pedro, who still lay under his net. I learned over and gripped his warm, frail body.

"*Hasta Nicaragua.*"

"*Hasta siempre.* Take care of yourself."

The backland is an apocalypse. The fields are burned and the red sun begins to rise over the blackened soil, almost hidden by the smoke.

When the sun is fiery hot, we will be cruising the Araguaia in Matos's launch and then boarding the plane for Brasilia. My last thoughts will be those that Pedro had impressed on my memory:

> It's time to face the new *imperium*
> With the ancient purple of the Passion.
> It's time to love unto death itself,
> To give the greatest proof.

—Postscript translated by John Drury

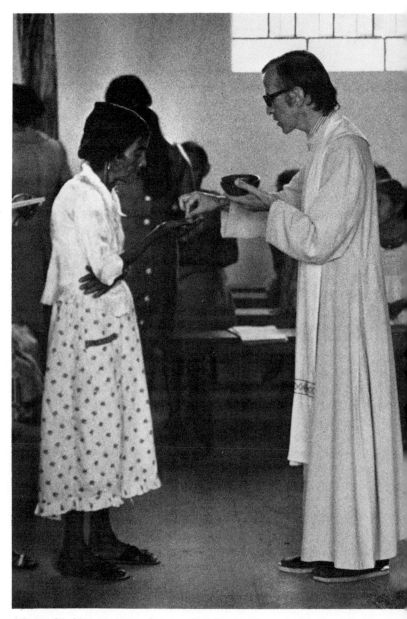

"I am thinking more and more that God will not judge us either for the good or the evil that we have done, but simply for whether we have been capable of accepting God's love and transmitting it to other people."

Notes

Introduction

1. Teófilo Cabestrero, *Faith: Conversations with Contemporary Theologians* (Maryknoll, N.Y.: Orbis Books, 1980). Interviews with L. Boros, G. Casalis, J. Comblin, E. D. Dussel, S. Galilea, G. Girardi, J. M. González-Ruíz, G. Gutiérrez, H. Kung. J. Moltmann, K. Rahner, J. Ratzinger, E. Schillebeeckx, J. L. Segundo, J. M. Tillard.

2. *Una iglesia que lucha contra la injusticia* [A Church that Struggles against Injustice] (Madrid: Misión Abierta, 1973).

3. Bilbao: Desclée de Brouwer, 1977; Eng. trans.: *I Believe in Justice and Hope* (Notre Dame: Fides Claretian, 1979).

4. Latin, "strictly so"; i.e., is the mass celebrated strictly as prescribed?

5. *Cauim* is a native Brazilian drink prepared from fermented manioc (a staple rootstock in the rural Brazilian diet). *Tapirapé* refers to the Brazilian Indians of the same name; see Chap. 5.

6. Latin, "nothing forbids" (i.e., the publication of a book); a formula certifying that nothing heretical has been found in a book submitted for ecclesiastical approbation.

7. Latin, "early in the morning of the first day of the week" (John 20:1), i.e., Easter Sunday morning.

Chapter 2

1. *¡Yo creo en la justicia y en la esperanza!*, pp. 117, 118.
2. Editorial Guadalupe, Buenos Aires, 1973.

Chapter 4

1. The cruzeiro, the basic monetary unit in Brazil, is worth approximately 45 cents, USA (May 1980).
2. A reference to Federico García Lorca (1899–1936), well known Spanish poet, whose work was filled with premonitions of death and who was in fact murdered.
3. The *Coplas a la muerte de su padre* [Verses on the Death of His Father] by Jorge Manrique (1440?–1479) are probably the most famous lines in Spanish poetry.

Chapter 5

1. A reference to Bartolomé de Las Casas (1474–1566), a Spanish Dominican priest, known as the Apostle of the Indies; he opposed the policy of giving land and Indian serfs to Spanish colonizers.

Chapter 6

1. Reference is to the Third General Conference of the Latin American Episcopate, Puebla, Mexico, January 27–February 13, 1979. For a discussion of the role of López Trujillo see John Eagleson and Philip Scharper, eds., *Puebla and Beyond* (Maryknoll, N.Y.: Orbis Books, 1980).

Chapter 9

1. Teófilo Cabestrero, *Los poemas malditos del obispo Casaldáliga* [The Cursed Poems of Bishop Casaldáliga] (Bilbao: Desclée de Brouwer, 1977).